George Wight

**Queensland**

The field for British labour and enterprise and the source of England's cotton supply

George Wight

**Queensland**
*The field for British labour and enterprise and the source of England's cotton supply*

ISBN/EAN: 9783337324650

Printed in Europe, USA, Canada, Australia, Japan

Cover: Foto ©Suzi / pixelio.de

More available books at **www.hansebooks.com**

# QUEENSLAND

THE FIELD FOR

BRITISH LABOUR AND ENTERPRISE,

AND THE

Source of England's Cotton Supply.

## Iron Roofs, Sheds, Houses, Churches.

## TUPPER & Co.'s
# CORRUGATED GALVANIZED IRON,
### FOR
### ROOFING, PATENT TILES, HOUSES, CHURCHES, SCHOOLS, &C.,

Packed for Shipment; also

### Gutters, Pipes, Ridging, Pails, Tubing, Wire, Nails, Screws, &c., all Galvanized.

*TUPPER & Co. furnish Designs and Estimates free of Charge.*

They supply, properly packed for Shipment, with all necessary Drawings and Instructions for erection abroad, every description of Iron Roofing, Iron Sheds, Stores, Houses, Churches, &c.; these are temporarily erected at the Iron Roofing Works in London, where they can be inspected prior to Shipment.

TUPPER & Co.'s Brands of Galvanized Corrugated Iron and their Patent Tiles are well known in the Australian, Cape, East and West Indian, and most Foreign Markets, as the best and cheapest.

**All Materials are guaranteed to be of the Best Quality.**

For Prices, Drawings, and Catalogues, apply at 61A, Moorgate Street, London, E.C., or Berkley Street, Birmingham.

*⁎* *Tupper & Co.'s Process of Galvanizing prevents Rust.*

## Offices, 61a, Moorgate Street, London.

## E. J. MONNERY & Co.'s
### New Zealand, Australian, and India
## OUTFITTING WAREHOUSE,
### 165, Fenchurch St., London, E.C.

*Canteen*

Hosiery, Shirts,
Waterproofs,
Flannel Shirts,
Sea Chests,
Overland Trunks.

*Drawers in two Parts.*

**SHOW ROOMS FOR CABIN FURNITURE.**
*Drawers in Two Parts with Cases to form Cupboards.*
**Canteens with all the recent Improvements.**

*Cabin Lamp*

Emigrants' Tents of every description, from £3 3s. upwards.

Emigrants' Cooking Stoves.

*Ship Table*

*Illustrated Price Catalogues free on application.*
**Passengers' Luggage Warehoused free of charge, and shipped if required.**

*Chair Bedstead*

*The same closed*

**ALL GOODS ARE DELIVERED FREE AT THE DOCKS.**

# E. J. MONNERY & Co.,
## Clothiers & General Outfitting Warehousemen
### TO ALL PARTS OF THE GLOBE,
### 165, FENCHURCH STREET, E.C.

| Bedding, &c., requisite for a First-Class Passenger. | | | | Bedding, &c., requisite for a Second-class Passenger. | | | |
|---|---|---|---|---|---|---|---|
| 1 Mattress and Pillow | £0 | 10 | 6 | 1 Mattress and Pillow | £0 | 7 | 6 |
| 2 Blankets | 0 | 9 | 6 | 2 Blankets | 0 | 7 | 6 |
| 1 Counterpane | 0 | 2 | 6 | 1 Counterpane | 0 | 2 | 0 |
| 4 Pair Sheets | 0 | 18 | 0 | 3 Pair Sheets | 0 | 7 | 6 |
| 6 Pillow Cases | 0 | 5 | 0 | 4 Pillow Cases | 0 | 3 | 0 |
| 1 Cabin Lamp | 0 | 8 | 6 | 1 Cabin Lamp | 0 | 3 | 6 |
| 6 lbs. India Wax Candles | 0 | 9 | 0 | 3 lbs. India Candles | 0 | 3 | 6 |
| 1 Wash Stand & Fittings | 0 | 12 | 6 | 1 Wash Stand & Fittings | 0 | 7 | 6 |
| 1 Looking Glass | 0 | 3 | 6 | 1 Water Can | 0 | 2 | 0 |
| 1 Camp Stool | 0 | 3 | 6 | 2 Knives and Forks | 0 | 2 | 0 |
| 1 Water Can | 0 | 4 | 6 | 2 Spoons | 0 | 1 | 0 |
| 1 Clothes Bag, with lock | 0 | 4 | 6 | 1 Hook Pot | 0 | 1 | 6 |
| | | | | 2 Enamelled Plates | 0 | 2 | 0 |
| | | | | 1 Ditto Drinking Mug | 0 | 1 | 3 |
| | | | | 2 Cups and Saucers | 0 | 2 | 0 |
| | | | | Dust Pan and Brush | 0 | 2 | 0 |
| | | | | Marine Soap | 0 | 1 | 9 |
| | £4 | 11 | 6 | | £2 | 17 | 6 |

| OUTFIT for 10s. 6d. | | | OUTFIT for 21s. | | | |
|---|---|---|---|---|---|---|
| Bed | | | Bed and Pillow | £0 | 5 | 6 |
| Hook Pot | | | 2 Blankets | 0 | 5 | 6 |
| Water Bottle | | | 2 Sheets | 0 | 2 | 0 |
| Wash Basin | s. | d. | Counterpane | 0 | 2 | 0 |
| Metal Plate | 10 | 6 | Hook Pot | 0 | 1 | 6 |
| Drinking Mug | | | Water Can | 0 | 1 | 6 |
| Knife and Fork | | | Wash Basin | 0 | 0 | 9 |
| Tea and Table Spoons | | | Metal Plate | 0 | 0 | 6 |
| 2 Sheets | | | Drinking Mug | 0 | 0 | 6 |
| Counterpane | | | Knife and Fork | 0 | 0 | 9 |
| | | | Tea and Table Spoons | 0 | 0 | 6 |
| | | | | £1 | 1 | 0 |

*Any of the above Articles can be had separate.*

**CABINS FITTED ON THE SHORTEST NOTICE.**

Lists of the Cabin Furniture, Clothing, &c., with Prices, Free on application.

*Baggage Warehoused free of charge, and carefully Shipped.*

## NOTICE TO PASSENGERS.

## AUSTRALIA AND NEW ZEALAND.

Before you decide upon your Cabin Furniture and Outfit, compare the prices and quality at JOHN SHEPHERD's Factory, 90, Bishopsgate Street Within, with other houses.

First Class Cabins fitted with every requisite for £4; Second Class, £1 15s.; Third Class, 20s.; also an Outfit for 10s. Established 1778.

All Furniture, Bedding, &c., supplied at the wholesale prices, and the cabins fitted and the goods carted free of charge. Packing cases 3d. per foot. Berths fixed, 6s. 6d.; Cabin Lamps, 5s. 6d.; Fibre Mattresses, 5s. 6d.; and every requisite equally low.

## JOHN SHEPHERD,
90, BISHOPSGATE STREET WITHIN, E.C.

# Australian Agency in London,
### 12, PALL MALL EAST, LONDON, S.W.

MESSRS. W. R. LOOKER & Co. beg to draw the attention of Colonists, or of those intending to settle in the Australian Colonies, to their Agency, now established four years. Much time, trouble, and expense, are saved by the employment of this Agency, and all commissions entrusted to them are executed with promptitude and care.

Private and general supplies of all descriptions purchased and shipped.

Letters of Credit, Bank Drafts, &c., provided. Dividends received and remitted, Banking Accounts opened, and every description of Monetary Business transacted.

Insurances effected, Life, Marine, or Fire.

Passages secured, Outfits arranged, Cabins fitted up, Baggage collected and shipped.

New Books, Periodicals, and Newspapers regularly forwarded.

Wool, Gold, and Colonial Produce generally, received on consignment and disposed of.

Purchase and Sale of all Colonial, British, and Foreign Securities effected promptly.

Letters, Parcels, &c., taken charge of and forwarded; an account of Postages kept and forwarded periodically.

# BANK OF NEW SOUTH WALES,

**ESTABLISHED 1817,**

*Incorporated by Act of the Colonial Legislature in 1850, and confirmed by Her Majesty in Council,*

## 37, CANNON STREET, CITY.

### CAPITAL £750,000.—RESERVE FUND £250,000.

THE BOARD OF DIRECTORS grant Letters of Credit, payable on demand, and Bills of Exchange at 3 and 30 Days' sight, on the undermentioned Establishments of the Corporation:—

### NEW SOUTH WALES.

| | | |
|---|---|---|
| Sydney. | Albury. | Deniliquin. |
| Maitland. | Goulburn. | Windsor. |
| Newcastle. | Mudgee. | Orange. |
| Adelong Agency. | Tamworth. | Penrith. |
| Bathurst. | | |

### VICTORIA.

| | | |
|---|---|---|
| Melbourne. | Wangaratta. | Ararat. |
| Geelong. | Ballarat. | Inglewood. |
| Tarrangower. | Sandhurst. | Creswick. |
| Kyneton. | Chiltern Agency. | Linton. |
| Castlemaine. | Beechworth. | |

### QUEENSLAND.

| | | |
|---|---|---|
| Brisbane. | Ipswich. | Toowoomba. |
| | Rockhampton. | |

### NEW ZEALAND.

| | | |
|---|---|---|
| Auckland. | Dunedin. | Napier. |
| Wellington. | Invercargill. | Kiapoi. |
| Lyttelton. | Nelson. | Timaru. |
| Christchurch. | | |

And also on the Commercial Bank of Van Dieman's Land at Hobart Town and Launceston.

The Directors also negotiate approved Bills of Exchange, and send them for collection, drawn on any of the Australian Colonies and New Zealand.

The Royal Bank of Scotland, Stuckey's Banking Company, the Manchester and Liverpool District Bank, the North and South Wales Bank Birmingham Joint Stock Bank (Limited), and the National Bank in Ireland, are authorised to grant Credits on this Bank at the several establishments in Australia, and will negotiate bills drawn on the Australian Colonies.

By order of the London Board,

JOHN CURRIE, *Secretary.*

# LONDON
# Chartered Bank of Australia,

INCORPORATED BY ROYAL CHARTER 1852.

---

### LONDON OFFICE,
## 17, CANNON STREET, CITY.

---

Paid up Capital . . . One Million.
Reserve Fund . . . . £60,000.

*Letters of Credit and Bills of Exchange are granted on the Branches of this Bank at*

### VICTORIA.

| | |
|---|---|
| MELBOURNE. | BALLAARAT. |
| GEELONG. | DUNOLLY. |
| ARARAT. | MARYBOROUGH. |

### SUB-BRANCHES.

TALBOT, LATE BACK CREEK.    MOONAMBEL, LATE MOUNTAIN
INGLEWOOD.    CREEK.
RED BANK.

### NEW SOUTH WALES.
#### SYDNEY.

---

Drafts on the Australian Colonies negotiated and sent for collection.

By order of the Court,
JAMES STRACHAN,
*Secretary*

# UNION BANK OF AUSTRALIA.

PAID-UP CAPITAL . . . £1,000,000.
RESERVE FUND . . . . £200,000.

THE DIRECTORS OF THIS BANK GRANT

## LETTERS OF CREDIT OR BILLS

At 3 or 30 Days' Sight, upon their Branches through the

AUSTRALIAN AND NEW ZEALAND COLONIES,

At the customary Rates, on the Money being deposited.

They also negotiate, or send for collection,

## BILLS ON THE COLONIES,

The Terms for which may be obtained on application at this Office.

(*Signed*) H. W. D. SAUNDERS,
*Secretary.*

**38, OLD BROAD STREET, E.C.**

---

## KAYE'S WORSDELL'S PILLS

ARE EVERYBODY'S MEDICINE, equally suited to Age and Infancy, Male and Female. Compounded of vegetable substances, they are free from the drawback of mineral drugs used by doctors, and may be taken with confidence under all circumstances. Medical men generally acknowledge that to

### PURIFY THE BLOOD

is to purge from disease, and this is the peculiar effect of KAYE'S WORSDELL'S PILLS. Being wholly vegetable, they cure in harmony with the laws of life, which mineral poisons violate. All, therefore, may take them with confidence as to their immediate effect, and without any fear of ulterior consequences. They are, indeed,

### HEALTHFUL AND HARMLESS,

and are applicable to every class of diseases in the human frame.

Country Householders, Emigrants, Colonists, and others, who desire speedy restoration and constant health, should never be without

### KAYE'S WORSDELL'S PILLS.

There is no ill that flesh is heir to which these Pills will not prevent or cure, if taken with perseverance.

Prepared solely by JOHN KAYE, Esq., of Prospect Hall, Woodford, Essex. Sold by all Chemists and other dealers in patent Medicines, at 1s. 1½d., 2s. 9d., and 4s. 6d. Wholesale depôt, 22, Bread Street, London.

Prize Medal, International Exhibition, 1862.

# KEATING'S COUGH LOZENGES.

JUDGED BY THE IMMENSE DEMAND, this UNIVERSAL REMEDY now stands the first in public favour and confidence; this result has been acquired by the test of fifty years experience. These Lozenges may be found on sale in every British Colony, and throughout India and China they have been highly esteemed wherever introduced. For COUGHS, ASTHMA, and all affections of the Throat and Chest, they are the most agreeable and efficacious remedy.

### IMPORTANT TESTIMONIAL.

*Copy of a letter from the late Colonel HAWKER (the well-known Author on "Guns and Shooting").*

"Longparish House, near Whitchurch, Hants.

"SIR,—I cannot resist informing you of the extraordinary effect I have experienced by taking only a few of your LOZENGES. I had a cough for several weeks that defied all that had been prescribed for me; and yet I got completely rid of it by taking about half a small box of your Lozenges, which I find are the only ones that relieve the cough without deranging the stomach or digestive organs.

" I am, Sir, your humble Servant,
"P. HAWKER.
"To Mr. KEATING, 79, St. Paul's Churchyard."

Prepared and Sold in Boxes, 1s.1½d., and Tins, 2s.9d., 4s.6d., and 10s.6d. each, by THOMAS KEATING, Chemist, &c., 79, St. Paul's Churchyard, London, and retail by all Druggists and Patent Medicine Vendors in the World.

## KEATING'S
# Persian Insect Destroying Powder.

THIS POWDER IS QUITE *HARMLESS* TO ANIMAL LIFE, but is unrivalled in destroying Fleas, Bugs, Emmets, Flies, Cockroaches, Beetles, Gnats, Mosquitoes, Moths in Furs, and every other species of Insects in all stages of metamorphosis.

SPORTSMEN will find this an invaluable remedy for destroying FLEAS IN THEIR DOGS, as also *Ladies for their Pet Dogs*, and sprinkled about the nests of Poultry, it will be found extremely efficacious in exterminating those Insects with which they are usually infested. It is perfectly harmless in its nature, and may be applied without any apprehension, *as it has no qualities deleterious to Animal Life.*

In Packets, post free for 14, or treble size for 36 postage stamps, by THOMAS KEATING, Chemist, 79, St. Paul's Churchyard, London, E.C.

N.B.—The above Medal was awarded to the Producer of this Powder.

# Colonial Books, Pamphlets, Maps, &c.
### SOLD BY
### G. STREET, 30, CORNHILL, LONDON.

|  | POST FREE. |
|---|---|
| "New Zealand, the Land of Promise" (Prize Essay) | 6d. |
| "Canterbury in 1862" (with Map) | 7d. |
| "Voices from Auckland" | 1s.2d. |
| "Hints to Sheep Farmers in New Zealand" | 9d. |
| "New Zealand, the Britain of the South" | 15s.6d. |
| "New Zealand Almanac" (current year) | 5s.4d. |
| "New Zealand, as it was and is" | 1s.2d. |
| "Queensland," by G. WIGHT | 3s.4d. |
| "Queensland," by Dr. LANG | 12s.6d. |
| "Western Australia" | 7d. |
| "Exploration of Interior of Australia" (Stuart's Diary) | 1s.1d. |
| "Settlers' Guide to the Cape and Natal" | 3s.10d. |
| "Natal," by Dr. MANN | 5s.6d. |
| "Canada, the Land of Hope" | 4d. |
| "Canada Almanac" (current year) | 1s.2d. |
| "Settlers' Guide to Canada" | 5s.6d. |
| "Prize Essay on Canada" | 4s.6d. |
| " " | 2s.4d. |
| "British Columbia" | 4d. |
| British Columbia, "Cariboo" | 1s.2d. |
| "Labour and its Wages" | 4d. |
| " " with Map of the World | 7d. |

Maps of New Zealand, at 1s.1d., 2s.2d., and 3s.8d., post free.
    ,,     Auckland (N.Z.) ... 1s.1d. ,,
    ,,     Canterbury (N.Z.) ... 10s.6d. ,,
    ,,     Queensland ... 7d., 2s.7d., and 4s.8d. ,,
    ,,     Victoria ... 4s.10d. ,,
    ,,     South Australia ... 7s.0d. ,,
    ,,     Canada (East and West) ... 2s.2d. ,,

### Colonial Summary Newspapers received for Sale by each Mail.

| | | | | £ s. d. | |
|---|---|---|---|---|---|
| "Melbourne Argus" | 7d. | ℔ copy, post free, or | 0 7 0 | ℔ ann. |
| "Sydney Morning Herald" | 9d. | ,, | ,, | 0 9 0 | ,, |
| "South Australian Advertiser" | 8d. | ,, | ,, | 0 8 0 | ,, |
| "Queensland Guardian" | 8d. | ,, | ,, | 0 8 0 | ,, |
| "Hobart Town Mercury" | 8d. | ,, | ,, | 0 8 0 | ,, |
| "New Zealander" (Auckland) | 10d. | ,, | ,, | 0 10 0 | ,, |
| "Wellington Advertiser" | 10d. | ,, | ,, | 0 10 0 | ,, |
| "Times of India" (Bombay) | 1s.1d. | ,, | ,, | 1 6 0 | ,, |
| "Calcutta Englishman's Weekly Mail" | 1s.1d. | ,, | ,, | 2 16 4 | ,, |
| "Cape Argus" | 7d. | ,, | ,, | 0 7 0 | ,, |
| "Natal Mercury" | 8d. | ,, | ,, | 0 8 0 | ,, |
| "Calcutta Directory" | 21s. | ,, | post free, 23s. | | |
| "Bombay Directory" | 15s. | ,, | ,, | 16s. | |

&c. &c. &c.

## The "NEW ZEALAND EXAMINER,"

A Monthly Journal of commercial and general information respecting New Zealand, published by G. STREET, 30, Cornhill, London. Price 5d. Post free, 6d. Annual Subscription, 6s.

## 1862.

# PRIZE MEDAL

#### AWARDED TO

## Ellwood's Patent Air-Chamber Hats & Helmets

#### THE ONLY

### Suitable Head-Dress for India.

Annexed is a section showing the principle by which the head is effectually protected from the rays of the sun.

SECTION.     SHOOTING HAT.

The Patent Air-chamber Hats and Helmets may be obtained by the Public of several of the principal Hatters, &c., in London and the chief towns of India, and by the Trade of the Patentees—

## J. ELLWOOD & SONS,

#### WHOLESALE MANUFACTURERS OF

## HELMETS AND HATS OF ALL KINDS,

### Great Charlotte Street, London, S.,

**WITHOUT WHOSE NAME ON THE LINING NONE ARE GENUINE.**

Under arrangements with Her Majesty's Government of Queensland.

 # BLACK BALL

## MONTHLY LINE OF CLIPPER PACKETS.

Free Grants of Land, value £30, are given to all Persons paying their own Passages by this Line.

*The only direct* REGULAR *Line of Queensland Packets.*

THE Ships forming the Black Ball Fleet are of world known reputation, are famous for their size, quick and regular Passages, and elegant accommodation, and the following form a part of those to be dispatched for the colony:—

| | | | |
|---|---|---|---|
| Wansfell | 1500 Tons | A1, at Lloyds. | |
| Montmorency | 1500 Tons | A1, | ,, |
| Saldanha | 3000 Tons | A1, | ,, |
| British Trident | 2500 Tons | A1, | ,, |
| Queensland | 1500 Tons | A1, | ,, |
| Young Australia | 1400 Tons | A1, | ,, |
| Solway | 1500 Tons | A1, | ,, |
| Vanguard | 1700 Tons | A1, | ,, |

## PASSAGE MONEY £18 AND UPWARDS.

Under arrangements with the Government of Queensland, T. M. MACKAY & Co., are prepared to receive applications for Free Passages to labourers, their wives, and families, being taken out by capitalists sailing in the above Vessels.

The above Line also dispatch their magnificent Clippers, whose accommodation for all classes of Passengers is unsurpassed, to Melbourne and Geelong, Sydney, Adelaide, Hobart Town, and Launceston, from London and Liverpool every fortnight.

For further Particulars regarding Queensland, apply to HENRY JORDAN, Queensland Emigration Commissioner, 17, GRACECHURCH STREET, E.C.; and for Freight or Passage, to Messrs. JAMES BAINES & Co., LIVERPOOL; to all Agents of the Black Ball Line; or to T. M. MACKAY & Co., 1, LEADENHALL STREET, LONDON, E.C.

## Portable Sugar and Cotton Machinery, &c.

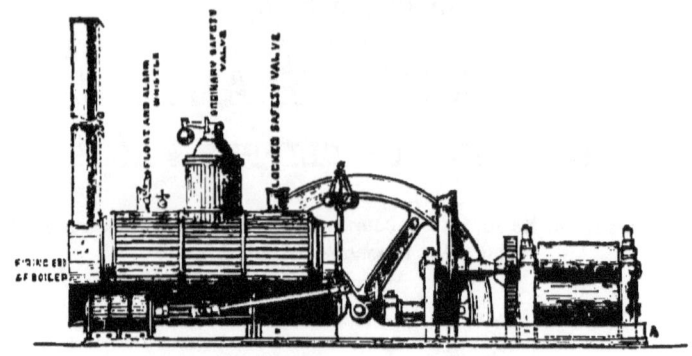

## A PRIZE MEDAL

AWARDED BY HER MAJESTY'S COMMISSIONERS, AT THE INTERNATIONAL EXHIBITION, LONDON, 1862.

REASONS FOR THE AWARD:—"*Portable Steam Sugar-Cane Mill.—Good Arrangement, Practical Utility, Good Workmanship.*"

## WILSON'S
# PATENT PORTABLE STEAM SUGAR-CANE MILL,

WITH Engine and Portable Boiler complete, on the same iron foundation plate. Expensive brick foundations and setting of boiler dispensed with. No brick chimney required. An additional saving effected from the simplicity of erection and economy of fuel. The smaller sizes are being extensively adopted instead of Cattle Mills. Prices and particulars free by post to intending purchasers.

Improved Sugar Machinery and Apparatus of all kinds. Cocoa-nut and other Oil Machinery. Coffee and Rice Machinery. Flax Steeping and Scutching Apparatus. Cotton Cleaning and Packing Machinery, &c.

### JOHN C. WILSON & CO.,
Colonial Engineers, 14a, Cannon Street, London.

\*\*\* *Order through Merchants, or J. C. W. & Co.'s Agents where established.*

Machinery at Work in the Western Annexe, Class VIII., International Exhibition.

# QUEENSLAND

THE FIELD FOR

# BRITISH LABOUR AND ENTERPRISE,

AND THE

# Source of England's Cotton Supply.

(WITH MAP)

By GEORGE WIGHT,

TWO YEARS AND A HALF RESIDENT IN THAT COLONY.

*Second Edition.*

PRICE 3s.  POST FREE 3s. 4D.

LONDON:
G. STREET, COLONIAL NEWSPAPER OFFICES,
30, CORNHILL.
1862.

"There is a tide in the affairs of men,
  Which, taken at the flood, leads on to fortune;
  Omitted, all the voyage of their life
  Is bound in shallows and in miseries.
  On such a full sea are we now afloat,
  And we must take the current when it serves,
  Or lose our ventures."

# NOTE TO SECOND EDITION.

In the Second Edition of this little work, so soon called for, the Author has nothing materially to alter or modify. There is only one side to a truthful description of a country. He has every reason to be satisfied with the reception it has met with from the public and from the press. It has been taken for what it was intended to be, and really is, nothing more than a plain, practical, trustworthy guide, for the industrious working man, to the great resources of a colony but little known to the British public before its appearance.

*August,* 1862.

# NOTE.

The reader of the following work on Queensland will speedily perceive that the writer has great faith in that colony, and that the terms in which he speaks of it are of the style generally called enthusiastic. It will be a pity should this feature of the book suggest to any one that the picture is overdrawn—that the prospect is too brilliant to be enduring; for in that case, my honest praise of one of the most productive of our many colonies, instead of encouraging, may discourage, the intending emigrant. I cannot speak of Queensland in other terms, for no other terms would be truthful; nor am I, in speaking thus, swayed by any mercenary consideration, for I have no connexion whatever with the Colonial Government, nor with any Emigration Agency in this country, nor do I expect to make a fortune by this book.

The truth of the matter is, and I wish every reader to know it, I have been induced to write this work from the deep interest I feel in the colony, and from a strong desire that has sprung up within me to place before my fellow countrymen the undeniable claims of this fine Field for the Surplus Labour of Britain.

I think the book opportune, appearing as it does when emigration to America is all but stopped, and when the important subject of Cotton Supply is attracting so much attention.

My aim has been to produce a work cheap and practical, containing as much of detail as may enable a sensible man, should he emigrate to Queensland, to work his way there with a fair prospect of success.

The Publisher presents with the work an excellent map, which should be freely used by the reader.

The book is commended to the candid perusal of the People, and I feel persuaded that the industrious man who may be induced by its statements to emigrate to that colony will never regret that he has exchanged the scanty pittance which, in many instances, his labour brings him in England, for the freehold farm and rough plenty that await him in Queensland.

MELROSE, SCOTLAND.

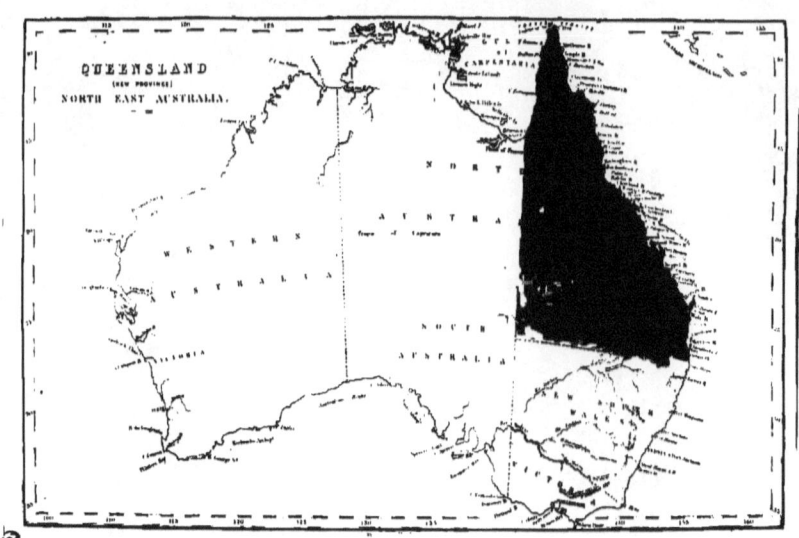

# CONTENTS.

| | | PAGE |
|---|---|---|
| I. | QUEENSLAND GEOGRAPHICAL | 1 |
| II. | ,, HISTORICAL | 6 |
| III. | PHYSICAL FEATURES | 16 |
| IV. | GEOLOGY | 25 |
| V. | CLIMATE | 29 |
| VI. | MOTIVES TO EMIGRATION | 37 |
| VII. | SQUATTING | 45 |
| VIII. | HOW TO SECURE A "RUN" | 50 |
| IX. | SQUATTING AND BRITISH LABOUR | 54 |
| X. | UPS AND DOWNS IN SQUATTING LIFE | 61 |
| XI. | A FEW DAYS ON THE PINE RIVER | 65 |
| XII. | THE DESIDERATUM | 75 |
| XIII. | WHAT WILL THE COLONY GROW? | 79 |
| XIV. | COTTON SUPPLY | 83 |
| XV. | QUEENSLAND COTTON-FIELD AND COTTON | 87 |
| XVI. | WHITE LABOUR, OR BLACK LABOUR, OR BOTH? | 93 |
| XVII. | OUR COTTON FARM | 104 |
| XVIII. | SUGAR, FLAX, FRUITS, AND OTHER PRODUCTS | 114 |
| XIX. | THREE DAYS IN THE BUSH | 123 |
| XX. | POPULATION, COMMERCE, REVENUE, AND BANKING | 131 |
| XXI. | THE DUGONG FISH—MEDICINAL QUALITIES OF ITS OIL | 139 |
| XXII. | QUEENSLAND POLITICAL AND SOCIAL | 144 |
| XXIII. | THE CHURCH, IN TOWN AND IN BUSH | 152 |
| XXIV. | EDUCATION | 157 |
| XXV. | EMIGRATION, EMIGRANTS, WAGES, HINTS, PRINCIPLES | 161 |

## APPENDIX.

| | |
|---|---|
| LAND GRANTS FOR COTTON CULTIVATION—ASSISTED EMIGRATION | 167 |
| OUTFITS AND VOYAGE NECESSARIES | 170 |

# QUEENSLAND:

## BRITISH LABOUR AND COTTON.

### I.—QUEENSLAND GEOGRAPHICAL.

In a book such as this, the object of which is to describe, as briefly as possible, a country which is but little known, and to direct attention to the resources of that country, which are at once varied and vast, we believe most readers will expect some account of its geographical position. Many books have been written on the Australian Colonies, and much is known of their character, climate, and productiveness; but of Queensland, a recent and vigorous offshoot from New South Wales, very little is known to the British public, and that little not always in the most accurate form. It has only to be known, however, to become rapidly one of the most attractive of all the colonies of Great Britain.

Some time since a volume on the colony of Queensland was published by the Rev. Dr. Lang, of Sydney, with which the present work is not intended to come into competition. I shall be content to place before the public the results of Two-and-a-half Years' Observation and Experience in Queensland, in such language as all shall understand, and at such a price as may enable every working man who has any idea of emigrating to possess himself of a copy.

Take the map of Australia, run your eye up the eastern coast, and you will observe, near latitude 28°, a promontory with an ominous name; and yet we know not whether this part of the Australian coast, more than any other, merits the unenviable designation. Indeed, no part between Port Jackson and Moreton Bay can be truthfully called "dangerous." The coast is low, but occasionally hilly and picturesque, creating an interest peculiarly its own; and rarely do the steamers, on their passage to and from Queensland, lose sight of land. The coral-reefs are first met with further north. The passage from Sydney to Brisbane, the capital of Queensland, is therefore a very pleasant one, and is performed by the steamers, that run weekly, in about fifty hours, including an awkward delay at Newcastle. The distance is within 500 miles.

Point Danger, in latitude 28° 8′, marks the boundary line between New South Wales and Queensland, and from this point the new colony, as at present constituted, stretches all the way to Cape York, the northern extremity of the great Australian continent, a distance of a thousand miles and more. The coast line is not hilly, but is sufficiently diversified to relieve it from the charge of sameness. It is coincident with the existence of the coral-reefs and the habitat of the dugong fish, a nondescript but valuable creature, of which some account will be given in a future chapter. On the south-west, the north-east point of South Australia bounds the colony in longitude 141°, 600 miles from the Pacific Ocean; whilst on the north, the Gulf of Carpentaria deeply indents the land, and bestows on these intertropical parts a rich soil and a salubrious climate.

The following extract from the Queen's Letters Patent, the Instrument by which the northern portion of New South Wales was erected in 1859 into an independent colony, furnishes the official definition of this land of promise. The language is vague as it regards the western boundary.

"Now know you, that We have, in pursuance of the powers vested in Us by the said Bill and Act, (a Bill to confer a constitution on New South Wales, &c.,) and of all other powers and authorities in Us in that behalf vested, separated from Our Colony of New South Wales, and erected into a separate Colony, so much of the said Colony of New South Wales as lies northward of a line commencing on the sea coast at Point Danger, in latitude about 28° 8′ south, and following the range thence, which divides the waters of the Tweed, Richmond, and Clarence Rivers from those of the Logan and Brisbane Rivers, westerly, to the great dividing range, between the waters falling to the east coast and those of the

River Murray; following the great dividing range southerly to the range dividing the waters of Tenterfield Creek from those of the main head of the Dumaresq River; following that range westerly to the Dumaresq River; and following that river (which is locally known as the Severn) downward to its confluence with the Macintyre River; thence following the Macintyre River, which, lower down, becomes the Barwan, downward to the 29th parellel of south latitude, and following that parellel westerly to the 141st meridian of east longitude, which is the eastern boundary of South Australia, together with all and every the adjacent Islands, the members and appurtenances, in the Pacific Ocean : And do by these presents separate from Our said Colony of New South Wales and erect the said Territory so described into a separate Colony, to be called the Colony of Queensland."

Queensland is at least nine times the area of England and Wales, and although it is, in all conscience, sufficiently large, yet there can be little doubt that the natural boundary on the south is not in latitude 28° 8′, but in latitude 30°. Had the dividing line been drawn here where it was originally intended, the new colony would have had within its boundary the fine agricultural districts of the Richmond and the Clarence. But although the adhesion of these districts would have been no small acquisition to the colony, as well as a certain advantage to themselves, yet it has within itself such vast and wonderfully varied resources, that it can well afford, should the Clarence men wish it, that this fertile region should remain an appendage to the parent colony.

But do the people wish it? This is the real question, according to the law by which the subdivision of the Australian colonies has hitherto proceeded. Many persons, especially in New South Wales, allege they do; while in the region itself it is well known that the people, according to the latest advices, are much divided in sentiment. Many desire a separate colony, which is never likely to be granted; an equal number, if not more, express a desire to be annexed to Queensland, an event which recent dispatches render improbable; and the merest fraction of the *bonâ fide* population remains true to its first love. Geographical position, climate, proximity to the capital and easy access thither, similarity of pursuits and political likings, all combine, however, in favour of annexation to Queensland.

But whatever may be the result of this agitation on the Clarence, few men doubt who are acquainted with colonial affairs, that, in process of time, another colony will be erected to the north of Queensland. For many reasons the city of Brisbane must remain the capital of the present colony. It is situated on the Brisbane, a river nearly a quarter of a mile broad, and capable, when the bar at its mouth, and two or three sandbanks in its course, have been removed, of carrying into the heart of the town any number of vessels drawing 22 feet of water. It is in the centre of an extensive cotton, sugar, tea, coffee, and fruit growing district; it is the natural outlet for the pastoral and agricultural products of the famous Darling Downs, and other far out-lying districts. Above all, the climate of Brisbane is the finest in all the Australias, and is the nearest approximation possible to that of Funchal, the capital of Madeira, the garden of the world. It would, of course, be the most consummate folly to abandon a capital possessing such advantages. But whilst the capital must remain where it is, it is not desirable that even the wisest and most practical body of Representatives whose place of concourse is on the banks of the Brisbane, should legislate for a population on the Gulf of Carpentaria, more than a thousand miles away. This would be the reproduction of the old and apparently ever new colonial grievance with a vengeance. We trust that Queensland, learning wisdom from New South Wales, will avoid this political blunder and social canker. As population increases, if it is of the right sort, and as the resources with which this country is blessed by a beneficent Providence become developed, the desire will certainly arise for a division of territory; and it would not surprise us though the present generation were to see another colony marked off to the north of Queensland, and another capital spring up somewhere on the healthy banks of the noble Fitzroy, or, perchance, on the River Burdekin, long deemed a myth, but now proved a reality.

The vague manner in which the western boundary line of the colony is described in the Letters Patent has given rise to a difference of opinion. The question is,—Whether did the official mind intend that the western boundary line of Queensland should be drawn *in continuation* of the east boundary line of South Australia, in longitude 141° onwards, till it cuts the Gulf of Carpentaria, leaving the country to the west of this line to New South Wales; or, did it intend that the Queensland boundary line on the west should run parallel with the South Australian boundary line *as far as it goes*, and then extend to the westward to enable it to include all known country in that direction, as the east and north boundaries extend to the sea?

The last interpretation of the official ambiguity is the most probable, although the Government of Queensland have wisely not acted upon it, but have referred the question for home solution.

The country to the west of Queensland, beyond the parallel of 141°, is that region that has been so recently explored by Stuart from South Australia. It is alleged by some that it should belong to South Australia, because the discoverer is a South Australian, and set out from Adelaide; but the absurdity of this notion is obvious, when it is known that the land in dispute is at least 1,200 miles from the seat of Government of South Australia, and the way to it is through the very heart of the continent. A claim is put in for New South Wales, and it is alleged that all the country to the west of 141° should be considered as belonging to the parent colony. This seems to us to be absurd also, because impracticable. This country is entirely cut off from New South Wales; and the only way to reach it, except by passing through Queensland, is to take ship, and double Cape York, steer through Torres' Straits, and disembark on the western shores of the Gulf of Carpentaria. Besides, that land was discovered *after* so much of the colony of New South Wales "as lies northward of a line commencing on the sea coast at Point Danger, in latitude 28° 8' south," was separated from the parent colony, and erected into the colony of Queensland. The fact is, the fine pastoral country discovered by Stuart lies naturally and inseparably into western Queensland, and no other colony can turn it to the smallest account. As a portion of Queensland, its resources will be gradually developed, as the Great Squatting Interest covers the land from the dividing range of mountains, about sixty miles from the Pacific, to the farthest west.

For the present, therefore, the immense country to the north and west, beyond Point Danger, and formerly belonging to New South Wales (virtually including the important discoveries of Stuart), constitutes the colony of Queensland, the capital of which is Brisbane, beautifully situated on the river of the same name, ten miles from the Bay as the crow flies, whence comes a genial sea breeze early in the day during all the hot months, with the regularity of sunrise, and welcome as the reviving breath of an English spring.

## II.—QUEENSLAND HISTORICAL.

The discovery of that part of the north-east Australian coast long known as Moreton Bay, and its external history, till the day when, by royal proclamation, it was constituted an independent colony, and assumed a recognised place among the members of Britain's colonial family, may be told in few paragraphs. There are no materials for history yet, but we believe that Queensland has entered on a career which will, in due time, secure to her a name and a place in the record of nations.

And yet, though ninety years have scarcely transpired since the great world-navigator, Captain Cook, anchored in the bay, this part of the globe has an inner history of no common import. For many years it was a penal settlement, a refuge for numbers of the most daring and desperate convicts that were ever landed on the Australian shores. That is now all over—over for years before the erection of the new colony; and the history of those times will never be written. There are, indeed, several persons still alive who remember the desperate characters of both sexes, and their "on-goings" in the "settlement," as the town was then called, and who could furnish ample raw material for as thrilling a chapter of human history as was ever put on record; but although you may occasionally succeed in inducing them to favour you with a yarn of the olden times, yet they will often meet your request with a shrug of the shoulder, and wind up by remarking that they can convey but a meagre impression of the then current state of matters.

In the middle of the month of May, 1770, Captain Cook cast anchor in the bay, into which debouches the River Brisbane, and several others of smaller dimensions, and of less commercial importance. It would appear that the navigator of the globe devoted little time and less care to the examination of the shores of the bay, otherwise it is hard to conceive that the indications of these fresh water outlets should have all been missed. On the occasion of the *Endeavour's* visit to these parts, an unfavourable wind is said to have prevailed, and to this cause the failure of the discovery of the leading features of this magnificent bay is ascribed. Captain Cook, however, attached to it the name by which it and the adjoining country have ever since been known, and which may stick to the country for a time, even after it has received the royal appellation of QUEENSLAND. The name, Moreton Bay, was given in honour of the Earl of Moreton, who was then President of the Royal Society. That the discoverer deemed Moreton Bay of trifling importance is obvious from the fact that in the narrative of his discoveries on the east coast of Australia, not more than twenty lines are devoted to the subject. Protected as the bay is from most winds, and from the heavy swell of the far Pacific by several islands, it strikes one as strange that a navigator of such experience and observation should have failed to discover a river that pours a body of water, a quarter of a mile broad, into the very centre of the bay.

For a period of nearly thirty years nothing was done by the Government of New South Wales, or any one else, to examine and fix the character of the northern coast. These were not times for much colonial enterprise, and the whole of north-east Australia, the most fertile and the most salubrious portion of all the continent, was left in the undisturbed possession of the indolent black savage, and his marsupial companion, the tawny kangaroo.

In the last year of the eighteenth century (1799), the representative of Majesty, Captain Hunter, the then Governor of New South Wales, was aroused from his dormancy, cast his eye northward, and actually sent an exploring party to examine the north-east coast, with the view of ascertaining whether there were any rivers in those parts of sufficient magnitude and draught to permit the ascent of small craft into the interior of this unknown land, that the way might be opened to British enterprise. Accordingly, Captain Flinders (then Lieutenant Flinders), a distinguished navigator, and the best man of the time for the expedition, was despatched to make a careful survey and examination of the coast, especially Moreton Bay and Hervey's Bay, some distance further to the north. Now, we may expect that what the unfavourable winds and other circumstances prevented Captain Cook from accomplishing, Captain Flinders will certainly realize. The most distinguished navigator of the time within reach of the Colonial Government, will surely discover the Clarence, the Tweed, the Logan, the Pine, or the Cabulture, all valuable rivers, and most of which fall into Moreton Bay, if he should by chance miss, as Cook had done, the entrance to the Brisbane. Not a bit of it! Not a river did he see; not a navigable opening did he find! Yes, I correct myself: he discovered "Pumice Stone River," which turned out to be a narrow creek between a small island in the bay and the mainland, and no river at all. This was the result of that well-intentioned, and, apparently, well-equipped expedition; and so confident was Captain Flinders that he had done his work well, that he closed his report to Governor Hunter with these words,—it is "an ascertained fact that no river of importance intersects the east coast between the 24th and 29th degrees of south latitude." There are, at least, a dozen navigable rivers in this space, among which are the Clarence, the Brisbane, the Mary, and the Burnett.

In other respects the results of this expedition were much more satisfactory. The exact position of many dangerous rocks and coral reefs was fixed, and the bearings of many points were accurately given. Captain Flinders is good authority in nautical matters, so far as the east coast of Australia is concerned, although since his day the surveys have been greatly extended and otherwise improved. On a subsequent expedition, undertaken early in the present century, Captain Flinders discovered Port Curtis, a bay that skirts a fine pastoral country, and a country, too, where the cotton plant flourishes luxuriantly.

The latitude is 24° south. The town of Gladstone, named after the present Chancellor of the Exchequer, stands on a small river that empties itself into Port Curtis.

Upwards of 20 years passed before anything more was done in the detailed examination of the coast to the north of Port Macquarie, a Penal Settlement in connexion with Sydney.

What neither the spirit of commercial enterprise nor the love of adventure could accomplish for the north of Australia, was brought about by the pressure of a motive more potent in those days,—the consideration of what was to be done with the ever-augmenting convict population. England had poured forth her incorrigible refuse in such numbers on the beautiful shores of Port Jackson, that after portions of the vile stream had been directed to Van Dieman's Land, to Norfolk Island, and Port Macquarie, the residue was more than could receive a decent lodgment in Sydney. A place was required where the most abandoned and desperate of this miserable class might be safely located, beyond the limits of the free population; and such a place it was hoped might be found in the far north.

Mr. Oxley, Surveyor-General of New South Wales, was selected as a proper person to carry out the intentions of the Government. He was accompanied by two or three other gentlemen, in H. M.'s cutter *Mermaid*. The party touched at Port Macquarie, from which place it was contemplated to remove the convicts, and to introduce a free population. On their way northward, they discovered the Tweed river, but seem to have passed Moreton Bay entirely, not touching the coast again till they had reached the 24th degree of south latitude. The date of this expedition was the close of 1823. The Boyne river was discovered and explored by Mr. Oxley at this time, after which he returned, and encountering a smart storm, ran into Moreton Bay. By a curious coincidence, the *Mermaid* anchored in Flinders' "Pumice Stone River," the narrow creek that separates the northernmost of the three islands that protect the bay, from the main land. Pumice Stone is found here in considerable quantities washed up on the beach; hence the name given to the supposed river.

Here the expedition met with and rescued some white men who had been carried in an open boat several hundred miles, and, after great privations, were cast upon this unknown shore, and exposed without the least protection to the tender mercies of the black savages. They were not, however, treated badly. It is probable that, previous to this disaster to the white men's boat, the aborigines of these parts had never seen a human being with a fairer skin than their own. No wonder that they looked upon them as superior beings.

The story of the castaways is substantially this:—A number of natives at the distance of a mile were observed advancing rapidly towards the cutter. The procession seemed friendly. On examining the crowd with the glass, it was remarked that one taller and lighter in colour than the rest walked in the midst of them. His copper colour looked fair when contrasted with the jet black skins of his companions. Great was the surprise and satisfaction of the exploring party when the copper-coloured savage hailed them in English.

The boat was immediately launched, and Mr. Oxley, with two of his party, went on shore. While approaching the beach, the natives gave proof of their friendly feeling in many demonstrations of joy, dancing their wild and peaceful dances, and embracing the copper-coloured with every evidence of cordial feeling. They were, of course, all in a state of nature, and the body of the Englishman was covered with white and red paint, obtained from certain clay deposits, and in general use among the blacks.

Thomas Pamphlet—for that was the name or nick-name of the copper-coloured—had left Sydney some six or eight months before, in an open boat, to fetch cedar from a place called the Five Islands, about 50 miles to the south of Sydney. There were three mates with him. Instead, however, of reaching their destination in the south, they had been carried out to sea, and, during a period of 21 days, in which terrible privations were endured, they had been tossed hither and thither, till at last they had been driven ashore on Moreton Island, near to the spot where the *Mermaid* was now lying, 500 miles north of their destination. One died of thirst on this terrible voyage; the other three survived.

Pamphlet was so bewildered with joy at the unexpected sight of the cutter and restoration to the society of white men, that he could give that night no connected account of his history and present condition. He was taken on board the

*Mermaid*, and the friendly blacks were left in wonderment on the beach, having had presented to them knives and handkerchiefs, as a tangible proof of the good feeling of the white men.

Re-assured by the kind treatment of Mr. Oxley's party, he told his tale, and the story, too, of his two companions, who, since they had reached the mainland, had parted company.

Richard Parsons and John Finnegan had, some weeks before, formed the desperate determination to make for Sydney through the trackless bush, a distance of which they had no conception, but which we know to be nearly 500 miles,—an undertaking the perils of which were so numerous, that they might well appal the stoutest heart. The home reader can form no conception whatever of travelling in the Australian bush without a guide, and without food, across creeks, and swamps, and rivers, and rough flinty hills, and through tribes of unknown tongue, and of filthy and, sometimes, cannibal habits. Yet I know a man who, within the last five years, has travelled on foot from Brisbane to Sydney and back without meeting with the slightest accident. He considers himself a "prophet of the Lord," and, verily, a kind Providence must have protected him.

All three set out for Sydney, their only guide being the short shadow of the meridian sun by day, and the pointer of the cross, the characteristic constellation of the southern hemisphere, by night. After travelling about 50 miles, Pamphlet's courage failed, and he tracked his way back to the place where he was found. In a few days Parsons and Finnegan quarrelled and parted; the latter made his way back to the friendly blacks; the former, like many poor wanderers on those southern shores, pressed onwards through the trackless bush, and was seen by the eyes of white men no more. Poor Parsons! our thoughts linger on the parting scene. Foot-sore, ill-clad, hungry, and angry, he disappears.

When Pamphlet was met with, Finnegan had gone with the chief of the tribe on a hunting expedition. In a few days he returned, and was rescued also by the *Mermaid*.

Mr. Oxley was informed by these two men, that, in their abortive attempt to escape from the intolerable society of even the friendly blacks of Moreton Bay, they had crossed a large and deep river, that emptied its waters into the bay, not a great distance from where the cutter was now anchored. Next morning a small party, headed by Oxley, and accompanied by Finnegan, started in the whale-boat to explore the river. It was found to be both deep and broad, bearing down an immense body of water, rising and falling with the flow and ebb of the ocean, and it received the name of the Governor of the time, Sir T. Brisbane.

It is, therefore, only 39 years since the Brisbane, one of the finest navigable rivers on the north-east coast of Australia, was discovered by these poor castaways, and explored by Surveyor-General Oxley.

In the year 1824, Moreton Bay was constituted a Penal Settlement, and the commencement was made at a place called Redcliff Point, on the main land, near the north end of the bay; but this soon appeared to be an unsuitable locality for such an establishment, and another spot was chosen on the banks of the Brisbane, 10 miles from the bay in a direct line, and nearly 15 miles by water. A more suitable place could not have been found in all these parts, and it now constitutes the site of the city of Brisbane.

When Redcliff Point was abandoned, the Government men left the buildings as a legacy to the blacks; but how the free and houseless sons of the soil appreciated the gift of their not over-scrupulous white intruders, may be conjectured from the title they bestowed on the deserted and dilapidated settlement. In their euphonious language they designated it "Humpybong," which may be freely rendered "Devil's House."

For 18 years Moreton Bay continued to be the receptacle of the most hopeless and wretched cases from Sydney, and came to stink in the nostrils of Englishmen like Botany Bay itself, till the public feeling of the colony, after having borne long with the huge grievance, could no longer be trifled with or resisted, and in 1842, this, the most recent of the Penal Settlements, was proclaimed free, and ready for the reception of a free population.

The convict settlement was in charge of a Commandant, and some inferior officers, whose functions partook not a little of the arbitrary and the despotic, and whose failings could scarcely be expected to lean to mercy's side. There were eight different commandants in succession, all of them military men; and it is alleged that some of them carried matters with a high hand, and directed them with a very weak head. Spread over these 18 sad years, there were ever and anon transpiring facts more wonderful than fiction, romances in real life, depravity brought to uncommon maturity, scenes of wanton oppression, at which nature revolts, and official blunderings of the most ludicrous and the most lamentable kind. But over these scenes, at which humanity weeps, and which, we trust, will never again be witnessed in this sunny land, we would draw the veil of deep oblivion, rejoicing meanwhile that the moral and social effects of that horrid system are being so rapidly and so thoroughly wiped away.

Many persons in England have the impression, that because Moreton Bay was once a Penal Settlement, therefore the white inhabitants of Queensland, if not the immediate descendants of convicts, must be deeply tainted with convictism. And this impression may possibly exist so extensively as to operate unfavourably as regards emigration to the country. This is not altogether unreasonable, as will be obvious to any person who has read the hurried historical sketch of Moreton Bay in these pages; but it would be altogether wrong were we to allow the shadow of such an impression to remain on the mind of the reader of this volume.

The 37,000 Queenslanders of this day are as free of the taint of convictism as the inhabitants of any of Her Majesty's Australian dominions; and it may be freer, as we hope to make it appear. Never was there a greater mistake; never was there a more groundless slander cast on a people than this.

There are, indeed, a few "old hands," as the Government emigrants of the olden time are called, but the proportion to the entire community is very small. I lived upwards of two years in the most densely-populated parts of the colony, and, in virtue of my profession, came much in contact with the people, and yet, during all that time, I met with very few who belonged to this class; and nearly the half of the number that I did know had been for years walking in the paths of virtue and religion, mainly through the efforts of that zealous and useful body of Christians, the Wesleyan Methodists.

Two causes have chiefly operated in purifying Queensland society from the taint of convictism. First,—Since penal times, there has been, for the number of liberated convicts, a large influx of free and well-to-do emigrants. Whenever men have come to know the real claims of that part of Australia, they have presently found their way thither. This, of course, if I may so speak, dilutes and sweetens the tainted element. Secondly,—Many of the liberated convicts were single, and have, since 1842, died out; and many more, ten years ago, were so bitten by the gold mania, that they betook themselves to the "diggings" in New South Wales and Victoria. Convicts are not generally the men to settle down and become permanent inhabitants anywhere, the least likely among the industrious and well conducted community that one everywhere meets with in Queensland.

In the autumn of 1857, the first steamer, appropriately called the *James Watt*, passed across the bay; now, the river steamers ply daily between Brisbane and Ipswich, a flourishing town on the Bremer, the chief tributary of the Brisbane river, and in convict times the "cattle station" to the settlement; once a week a large-sized steamer runs to and from Sydney, and once a fortnight from Brisbane to the ports on the north-east.

The country was now being explored, and important discoveries were being made, and the great Squatting Interest began to introduce its flocks and its herds to the extensive and well-grassed downs and plains that lie beyond the mountain ranges that form the backbone of the colony.

In 1843 Moreton Bay may be said to have commenced its political existence, as it was in that year that the country to the north of the 30th degree of south latitude returned one member to the House of Assembly in Sydney. Eight years later, Moreton Bay had a member of her own to represent her interests in the New South Wales assembly; and two years later still (1853) it had two. The number was still further increased in 1855, and, in 1858 the Electoral Bill gave nine to that part of the vast colony of New South Wales. This Act was in operation when separation took place in 1859.

Till 1851, the colony of New South Wales included the whole of the eastern portion of the continent from Bass' Straits on the south to Cape York on the north, although beyond Moreton Bay, rarely had the foot of a white man penetrated. There was, indeed, an attempt made in the year 1846-7, under the auspices of Lord Stanley (now Earl of Derby), to establish a new convict colony to the north of the 26th degree of south latitude, that is, about 120 miles beyond Brisbane, the capital of which was to be very near the tropic of Capricorn; but after an ignoble existence of a few months, it became a thorough failure. In the year above named, 1851, the spirited inhabitants of Port Philip effected a separation from the parent colony, and had conferred upon them an independent political constitution, under a Governor, Assembly, and Council of their own.

The causes that had led to the establishment of Victoria on the South, the men of the north believed were as good to justify them in demanding separate political existence also; and so the same year that saw the agitation succeed at Port Philip, saw it begin at Moreton Bay. Dr. Lang was one of the first to ventilate this question when on a visit to the north; and no man had done more, since Moreton Bay had been opened to free emigrants, than he, to induce the proper families to come. He was admirably assisted in the political and social struggle for independent existence. Many good men and true kept at the work of agitation, with intervals of repose, for eight years, before their arguments told, and the prayers of their petitions to the throne were answered. At last, the utmost efforts of the enemies of separation were exhausted, and Her Majesty graciously granted the boon, and condescendingly gave to our colony its new name. On the 10th of December, 1859, Moreton Bay, with all to the north of Point Danger in latitude 28° 8′ south, was proclaimed as the new colony of—

QUEENSLAND.

The arrival of the first Governor, Sir George Ferguson Bowen, and the proclamation of the independence of Queensland, occurred on the same day. The reception given to His Excellency was most loyal, and could scarcely be surpassed for genuine cordiality. All Brisbane, and a large portion of Ipswich, and many of the lieges from great distances, turned out in holiday attire; and as the steamer, that bore the first representative of royalty from the bay, whither he had come from Sydney in H. M. S. *Cordelia*, neared the landing-place in the heart of the city, the sight from the deck was very imposing. The day was magnificent, the river was swarming with gaily bedecked craft, and on the green banks there stood thousands to welcome the august stranger. The first favourable impressions produced by the open, manly, and cordial manner of Sir George F. Bowen, have, after a twelve months' political campaign, lost but little of their vividness.

## III.—PHYSICAL FEATURES.

There are countries where the rivers are broader and longer, where the mountains are higher and grander, than in Queensland; but there are few countries where the rocks are more auriferous, the plains better suited for pasture, the soil more varied and productive, and the climate more salubrious.

An extensive mountain system of moderate height runs through the colony from south to north, the continuation of the central range of New South Wales, and is cut off by the trending of the northern land towards Torres' Straits. The Dividing Range, as the mountains are called by the colonists, runs nearly parallel with the Pacific, at a distance of from 70 to 50 miles. On the west of the main range, many secondary ones run in all directions, diversifying and beautifying the extensive country that stretches away for hundreds of miles, and rendering it most valuable pasturage for the ever-growing flocks and herds of the Squatter. Here are the sources of numerous streams, that converge into several large rivers, and drain the country of its superfluous water in the wet seasons, and furnish innumerable water holes for the supply of man and beast when the seasons are dry. The country spreads out into magnificent plains and downs, thinly timbered, well watered, and covered with an abundance of feed for innumerable flocks of sheep, cattle and horses; while on the east or sea-board side of the mountains, many spurs push themselves down into the low country. Many isolated hills rise picturesquely from the plains, and broken or hilly country abounds. Generally speaking, this part of the country is heavily timbered, well grassed, and nearly all of it fit for cultivation.

Over the thousand miles of coast, many rivers, several of them navigable for many miles, intersect the country, and contribute largely to its fertility and its beauty.

Queensland is a fair and a good land, pity it is that there are so few to drink in its beauties and share in its untold riches. Let not the smile of credulity curl the lip; say not, "It is thus that every enthusiastic spirit speaks regarding the land of his adoption, wherever or whatever that land may be." Mark me, I speak soberly what I have seen and experienced; and when you have reached the close of this volume, if you should not feel that I have made out my case in favour of Queensland, as one of the finest fields for the industrious, good-principled British workman, where he is certain to meet with a speedy and substantial reward for his labour, which is his capital,—why, then, no one will compel you to go there; but if, on the contrary, you should feel that the case is proved, that Queensland is, in point of fact, all that we assert it to be, and, perhaps, somewhat more,—why, then, you will arise, consult with your wife, "bundle and go." The honour is greatest to him who helps to lay well the foundations of a country; the prizes are highest in value, more numerous, and easiest won, when the well-equipped competitor early enters the field.

Queensland is divided into seven large districts; and it may be advisable to follow the common enumeration of these, in placing before you a rapid survey of the physical features of the country. I shall not weary the reader by transcribing long and heavy documents descriptive of the country,—its rivers, or its mountains, or its vast plains, or its rich cotton and sugar soils. Condensation is my aim, and I shall do my utmost to give a faithful report.

### Moreton

Is the district first met with, and first in importance. It skirts the bay of the same name, and stretches inland to the Dividing Range. It occupies the south-east portion of the colony. Along the coast it is flat and unpicturesque, but inland it assumes a more hilly and broken appearance. By far the greater part of the inhabitants are scattered over this district, and about the centre of it stand the two principal towns in the colony—Brisbane and Ipswich. Large portions of the soil are black alluvial deposits, and rich plateaux of deep red colour; while the major part is light and well-adapted to the growth of cotton, sugar, tea, and fruits of various kinds. Portions are fitted only for grazing, but all is useful. It is well watered, having, within a coast line of 100 miles, six rivers, five admitting of the passage of small craft a number of miles up the country, and one—the Brisbane—navigable, with its tributary, the Bremer, for 50 miles. When the dredging machine has done its work at the mouth of the river, the largest ships that sail from London or Liverpool may cast anchor within the boundary of the city of Brisbane.

It was late on a Saturday night, in the month of May 1858, when the steamer *Yarra Yarra*, in which I had come from Sydney, cast anchor under the lighthouse at Cape Moreton, the entrance to the bay. In the morning I was up with the sun, anxious to catch the first glimpse of the land that I had chosen as my home for the remainder of my days. What a scene spread itself before me! The bay, with its numerous islands, and its margin of deep green, lay in the sweetest repose. The morning was cloudless, and as the golden light of the newly-risen sun glinted athwart the vast expanse of waveless waters, and fell soft and rich on the far-extending densely-wooded coast, I felt that the eye could not look on a scene more beautiful, and more in harmony with the blissful Sabbath morn.

The bay is about 60 miles long, by about 20 miles in breadth. On the side of the Pacific it is bounded by three islands in continuation, whilst numerous small islands, all covered with vegetation, diversify its surface. As we approached the land-side of the bay, it became obvious that the low coast, as far as the eye could reach, was covered quite to the water's edge with the sombre, unvarying mangrove, while deep indentations suggested to the unpractised beholder the openings of creeks, or the estuaries of rivers. These blind creeks, as they are called, lead to nowhere, but terminate in mimic bays of black mud, fringed, even below high water mark, with the never failing mangrove. The coast is in the process of rising by degrees which cannot be measured by human arithmetic; we know it only by the "bars" that stretch across its rivers, and the mud-deposit that is found between high and low water mark.

It was 11 A.M. before the state of the tide admitted of our

crossing the bar at the mouth of the Brisbane. Whilst waiting outside, under the glare of the now powerful sun, we were much interested and amused with several birds of the hawk species that came off from the land at our approach, and perched on the beacons that marked out the channel for the ships. As the *Yarra Yarra* floated easily, her steam escaping with a hissing sound, our feathered visitors sat with their faces towards us in ludicrous imperturbability. How solemn they looked, those strange birds! If, in their case, instinct passes into reason, one would be curious to know what might be their cogitations as the little steamer puffed and blew like a great sea monster.

The banks of the river at its mouth are very low, only a few inches higher, apparently, than the daily tides rise, and are densely covered with mangrove. On the sand banks, where the water was shallow, scores of pelicans were feeding leisurely on the fish, that appeared to be very abundant. They had odd ways with them, those birds, at least it struck me they had. Sometimes they would walk in Indian file, and feed as they went; at other times they would scatter themselves abroad, and feed apart. Their step was slow and majestic, and the eye was fixed steadily on the water. Many a luckless fish was "pocketed" that day, if the frequency with which they plunged their long bills in the water might justify us in drawing inferences.

At intervals, narrow creeks break off from the main channel, and form a labyrinth of waters among the dense, and now varied vegetation. Here is the home of wild duck and fish, and many a day's sport with rod and with gun has it yielded to the few Brisbanites who have the time or the taste for such aqua-sylvan amusements. The banks now become higher, drier, and better defined, and the timber and vegetation much more varied and interesting, albeit an Australian forest is never *very* interesting. The forest, or bush, is tame, uniform, for ever the same endless waste of gum-trees, making all but shepherds and stockmen miserable, and many of *them*, too, we should find, were they to favour us with their experience; the scrub only is beautiful, that is, the dense vegetation that grows on the alluvial banks of rivers and creeks.

There on a grassy knoll, a group of aborigines is squatting in the sun. They rise and salute us as we pass. In the distance they appear fine specimens of the black race, and impress the mind more favourably than their sable brethren whom I had seen 600 miles further south.

Onwards we steam, and now cleared patches are met with, on which wooden houses have been erected, and maize and vegetables, and fruit are being cultivated. We are approaching the small farms, only as yet under partial cultivation, belonging to the settlers that have in this direction gone furthest from the town.

The river in all its magnificence spreads before us, and the view a-head is one of growing extent and richness. Villas peep out from quiet corners, and from the bow of the steamer is seen the beautiful residence of Captain Wickham, R.N., the then Government Resident at Moreton Bay, perched on a green promontory formed by the junction of Breakfast Creek with the river. In the distance the eye rests on the wooded heights of Taylor's Range, a granite formation, some miles beyond Brisbane, and then pierces far into the open country.

The town itself was yet hid from view by the spacious windings of the river among low, undulating ridges, that render its environs peculiarly beautiful and healthy. We catch a momentary glimpse of Fortitude Valley, the northern portion of the city. The reaches of the river, as they open and close, with their surface smooth as a mirror, and reflecting the shadows of the trees that hang over their margins, remind one of some of the most lovely of the Scottish lochs.

The villas become more frequent and more tasteful, indicating our approach to the town; and there, at last, is Brisbane, the capital of the North. From the deck of the steamer it is impossible to describe it, as the river winds through its very heart, like some great life-artery, as it is, both in a commercial and sanitary point of view. Like all new colonial towns, it is straggling, and ill put together. Much grass, and many stumps of trees, are yet to be found within its proscribed limits; but the central streets contain some good buildings, and along the high grounds are many commodious and pleasant residences. There is the pleasant bustle of an embryo trading community; and altogether you have the conviction that Brisbane will flourish. Unlike many colonial towns, its site is unsurpassed for beauty and utility by any in the Australias.

It was Sunday, and the good people of Brisbane were just leaving morning service. Groups of well-dressed persons were passing quietly along the grassy streets; some families were gliding down the river in boats to their homes on its banks; while not a few found their way to the quay where we were now moored. The arrival of a steamer is a great occasion to the inhabitants of a small colonial town. I shall never forget that day and that scene, as I paced the deck of the little steamer alone, after all my shipmates had taken their departure, "a stranger in a strange land." Nevertheless, my first impressions of the place were favourable, and long ere sunset I had ample proof of the hospitality of the people.

The district of Moreton is better adapted for the depasturing of cattle and horses than sheep; and the portions of it that border the coast and skirt the rivers are capable of producing cotton, sugar, tea, fruits, &c., of the finest quality, and at highly remunerative rates.

### Darling Downs

Constitute the second district, immediately to the west of Moreton, and divided from the latter by the great mountain range, about 4,000 feet above the level of the sea, and 75 miles from Brisbane. Mount Lindsay, on the southern boundary line, the highest peak in the M'Pherson range, and not many miles from where Moreton and Darling Downs meet, is nearly 6,000 feet high.

This district is much more extensive than that of Moreton, and, with the exception of some patches of land on its eastern margin, is entirely devoted to pastoral purposes. As a sheep country, it is famed all over the colonies, and wherever wool is used as a staple. It is one magnificent sheep-run, with small nuclei of population at wide intervals. The country is composed chiefly of plains and downs of dry black soil, with flats in some parts, that become flooded in wet weather, and mountain ridges, that mark its boundary, and divide its plains. The downs are covered with herbage admirably adapted to sheep, and which is luxuriant even in winter. The hills are heavily timbered with gum-tree, stringy-bark, pine, &c., but, notwithstanding, produce, among the trees, even to their summits, a rich grass. The entire district is well watered, and possessed of every attraction to the breeder of sheep and the producer of wool. This fine district was discovered by the late Mr. Alan Cunningham, in 1827, and the one practicable defile by which the downs are reached from the east bears the name of "Cunningham's Gap."

Many streams have their sources in the high lands, and, on the south, a river called the Weir falls into the Macintyre River, the dividing line between New South Wales and Queensland; but the great river that drains the downs is the Condamine. Its course is first north, then westerly, then west, till it bends round and flows in a south-westerly direction almost in the form of a half circle. On its banks there is much scrub, and, therefore, much fine rich soil awaiting the coming of the agriculturist. Near latitude 27° south, the Condamine enters the district of

## MARANOA:

And from this point it receives the name of the Malonne. The Maranoa lies due west from the Darling Downs. Its eastern boundary is near 149° east longitude, and it may be supposed to stretch to the parallel of 141°. Only a small portion of this immense country has been explored, and a smaller portion still taken up by the adventurous squatter. It returns one member to the Queensland Assembly, and the Darling Downs District returns two. Little, therefore, is known of the Maranoa; we know, however, that it too is a good pasture country, rewarding the squatter for his labour and expense in driving his flocks so far inland. The country is partly hilly and broken; but vast tracks are level, and covered with vegetation of a rich character. Along both banks of the Malonne, and many miles off, there are scrubs of great extent, great beauty, and impenetrable denseness. These dark and dense thickets become the home of wild cattle, and form an impregnable stronghold for unfriendly blacks. As yet the Maranoa is destitute of anything in the shape of an agricultural or town population, and, for a long while to come, it will remain the "squatter's own" in undisturbed possession.

## LEICHHARDT

Joins the Maranoa on the north, and also the portion of the Darling Downs beyond the Condamine, the boundary between being the Main Range, and, in a north-westerly direction, the mountains known by the name of Denham Range. The district takes its name from the great Australian explorer, who, after having explored and described much of the interior of what is now Queensland, made yet another effort to penetrate still further, and never returned to tell the tale of his privations and his discoveries. Whether he fell by the hand of the savage or died of disease, or dropped on some arid plain a martyr to thirst and hunger, it is not given us to know. Every effort to find him, or even to trace his course for any distance beyond the most advanced station, proved a failure, and his fate is reluctantly left an insoluble mystery. Much of this country is high land, with extensive and well-conditioned plains and valleys. The drainage falls into the centre of the district, and finds its way through the mountains to the east coast. The river-system of the Leichhardt is on a large and complicated scale. In the numerous spurs of Denham Range are the sources of the Dawson, a river famous for the tragedies that have been perpetrated by the blacks on some of the white families that have penetrated so far. After flowing east, and gathering a large body of water from numerous streams and creeks, it takes a northerly direction, and continues its course till it reaches the tropic of Capricorn. In the high lands of the far north in about latitude 21°, the river Isaacs takes its rise, and flows in a south-easterly direction towards the course of the Dawson. The vast country that is bounded by these two water-sheds becomes mountainous in its western division; and there, among these western uplands, other two rivers take their rise,—on the south, or Dawson side, the Comet, and on the north, or Isaacs side, the Mackenzie. The Comet is absorbed in the Mackenzie, near to the tropic; and the Mackenzie itself loses its identity in the Isaacs, in latitude 23°. The waters of the Dawson from the south, and the waters of the Isaacs from the north, after losing not a little of their volume by evaporation, combine and form the Fitzroy, which empties itself into Kepple Bay.

We have arrived on the east coast again, after a rapid tour through the boundless pasture lands of the colony, to the west of the great Dividing Range, but at a point much further north than that from which we started. We are now under the tropic of Capricorn, and the heat of the sun is very powerful, though moderated by the constant breeze from the Pacific. Kepple Bay is the principal sea-port of the

### Port Curtis District;

But the town, Rockhampton, is a number of miles up the river Fitzroy. Gladstone is also a sea-port, and although favoured and fostered in old times, seems to succumb to its rival under the new state of things. The district is hilly, if it cannot be called mountainous, but contains a large quantity of fine agricultural land. It is watered by various streams, the principal rivers being the Boyne, the Caliope, and the Fitzroy. The gold field, to which thousands flocked from the southern colonies two or three years ago, and where so many met with biting disappointment, lies on the Fitzroy, 40 miles above Rockhampton.

Two districts remain to be described, the one to the north and the other to the south of Port Curtis. We shall take the southern district first.

### The Burnett,

or Wide Bay, lies geographically between Port Curtis and Moreton, and is surpassed in some respects by neither. Inland its physical character is decidedly hilly, sometimes mountainous, but abounding in fine pasture. Along the coast the country is equal to any in the colony for agricultural purposes, especially for cotton and sugar. The principal rivers are the Mary, on which the thriving town of Marybourgh, the port of the district, is being built, and the Burnett which waters by its innumerable tributaries, the whole of the high lands. It falls into Hervey's Bay at a bare and exposed part of the coast.

The most recently explored and defined district of Queensland is that of

### Kennedy.

Leichhardt traversed the inner portion of this district on his way to Port Essington, sixteen years ago, but the coast line was involved in so much uncertainty, that not till the detailed examination of Dalrymple and others, and the discovery of the mouths of the Burdekin, was it proclaimed a district fit for the reception of emigrants. This was done only a few months ago by the Governor of Queensland, in council; and it received the name of an unfortunate explorer who was speared to death by the unfriendly aborigines. The documents that have been published regarding the Kennedy show that it is a country admirably adapted to pastoral purposes. It is of immense extent, and is watered by the Burdekin, some of the branches of which were crossed by Leichhardt, but which was long deemed a myth, and now at last is proved to be a reality, a huge body of running water, with some half dozen outlets. The mouths of the river are not navigable for large ships. Port Denison is the harbour, in Edgecombe Bay, in the 20th degree of north latitude. The sea-board of this district alone is upwards of 300 miles, and its width upwards of 200 miles. Many of the tributaries of the Burdekin are themselves large rivers, and much fresh water from the Kennedy, as well as from all the districts, must disappear by absorption, and the constant process of evaporation.

Brief though this description be of a subject so large and so inviting, yet the reader will have no difficulty in gathering from it that little of the land of Queensland, so far as yet known, is barren and useless; that the entire colony is adapted to the uses of the sheep and cattle farmer; that millions of acres on the sea-coast, by the banks of rivers and creeks innumerable, are of the highest agricultural value; that excellent timber for all purposes everywhere abounds, but not in such quantities where agriculture will be most extensively followed, as to operate against that department of labour; that everywhere rivers and navigable creeks intersect the agricultural lands, thus forming ready-made highways for the removing of all kinds of produce to the coast, or to the centres of population.

Having spoken of the surface of the country, for the sake of those readers who might be curious to know a little of what is beneath the surface, I shall devote a section to its geology.

## IV.—GEOLOGY.

The non-scientific reader will not be scared away by this announcement, as even he may like to know whether this good land possesses any of those stores that constitute the mineral wealth of England, and that abound in the three Southern Australian colonies.

Limited districts only of the colony have been examined geologically with scientific care; and all we know of the other parts is gathered from the remarks, sometimes casual, and always the result of brief examination, of the various explorers that have penetrated the interior, such as Oxley, Lockyer, Cunningham, Kennedy, Mitchell, Leichhardt, and Gregory, the present Surveyor-General of Queensland. And even though there had been a greater abundance of trustworthy material, yet it would not have been in accordance with the plan of this popular work, to have written largely on the subject.

As in all mountainous regions where the older rocks prevail, granite is found, though not in such continuous masses as in some parts of the globe. Sometimes it forms the highest part of the mountain; but more frequently it forms the base, on which is elevated an apex of some other igneous rock. It abounds more in the interior than on the sea-ward side of the Great Range, yet I have met with it *in situ* less than 20 miles from the coast.

Igneous rocks of the trappean and porphyritic types exist in vast abundance all over the colony, and mingle curiously with each other, and with rocks of a sedimentary origin. In a few sentences, and without the use of diagrams, it is quite impossible to convey an accurate conception of these co-mingling masses. Mr. Alan Cunningham says of the main Range, where the great inland road crosses for Darling Downs and Maranoa, that "the base is of a compact whinstone; on the higher ridges were observed amygdaloid, or the trap formation, with nodules of quartz, whilst the summit exhibited a porphyritic rock, very porous, and containing numerous minute quartzose crystallizations."

For the following paragraphs I am indebted to an article in the *Queensland Guardian*, of December 22nd, 1860. The writer is obviously well acquainted with the subject, so far as accurate and extensive acquaintance could be gained with the scanty materials at his disposal:—

" In the first instance, it may be premised, that Queensland consists of several parallel ranges of hills, the general direction trending north and south, the strata having a dip to the westward, and thus showing steeper escarpments on the eastern than on the western sides of the ranges, while the elevation of the eastern ranges is greatest, rising to 5,000 feet near the coast, and the undulations gradually decrease on proceeding westward till they subside into the nearly level plains of the desert interior. Granite is not largely developed, but is frequently found forming the eastern bases and lower hills of the ranges near the coast, at intervals along the whole line from Taylor's Range, near Brisbane, to the head of the Burdekin, on which river it is more largely developed than in the more southern districts. Thick beds of coarse slate, which are intersected by small quartz veins crossing it in all directions, are the next in succession, and, resting on the granite, forms many of the higher hills and elevated country within 100 miles of the east coast. This rock is the source of the deposits of gold which have been found so widely diffused over the country already prospected over, although hitherto with little success as regards profitable gold-fields, though this may be in some measure attributed to the dissimilarity of the circumstances under which gold occurs in the northern portions of Australia as compared with the southern fields in Victoria; thus the gold miner from the latter place seeks for stony ridges with quartz, as an indication of the precious metal, which is usually confined to the black soil that results from the decomposition of the serpentine rock forming the matrix of the metal, which usually lies near its original position, not having been acted on by the violent currents which seem to have deposited the rich loads of gold in the deep sinkings to the south.

"Of equal importance with the auriferous deposits in the slates of the eastern coast, may be ranked the copper veins, about 23 miles west of Gladstone, which, from the richness of the ore (an oxide yielding 40 per cent. of pure metal), and the proximity of the commodious harbour of Port Curtis, give promise of a source of wealth that may prove even more permanently profitable to the community than mines of the nobler metal.

"Vast masses of porphyritic rock have been erupted through fissures in the slates, and form some of the higher summits of the great range dividing the eastern waters from those flowing towards the interior, as at Cunningham's Gap, on the road from

Brisbane to Warwick, and many of the hills on the western side of the Burdekin river; but like most of the older eruptive rocks, it presents few important features in other parts of the colony.

"With the exception of some small patches of limestone appearing to underlie the carboniferous rocks, the next of importance in the system are the coal-bearing strata, which are so largely developed as to form the chief feature of the territory under consideration (the south-east coast). The lower portion of the series consists of shales and seams of coal, of various thicknesses and qualities, some of which are already worked to advantage on the banks of the Brisbane river, and supply the steamers employed on our coast and rivers with fuel little inferior to that produced by the mines on the Hunter river, near Newcastle. Excellent freestone is also abundant in this part of the series of strata; but far the most important feature regarding it is the extensive development of the softer shales, forming the fertile plains of the Darling Downs, Fitzroy Downs, the Dawson, Peak Downs, and the heads of the Isaacs' river, in all of which places coal is found associated with basaltic rocks, which have burst forth and formed ridges and table lands, affording excellent pasture, while it occasionally rises into important masses of hills, as the Dividing Range, near Drayton, and Buckland Table Land, rising to 3,000 feet above the sea level. The basaltic rocks are, however, chiefly developed on a line parallel to the coast, about 100 miles inland, and extending from Warwick to the head of the Burdekin, in latitude 18 degrees.

"Proceeding eastward, the upper sandstones of the carboniferous series cover to a greater extent the argilaceous shales which predominate in the lower part, and the fertility of the country consequently decreases until it subsides into a nearly level plain of coarse ferruginous sandstone, covered with a bed of red sand or loam, formed by the decomposition of its surface."

The numerous islands skirting the coast are largely covered with loose sand, and yet, in such a climate, the vegetation even there is, in many instances, wonderfully luxuriant.

Volcanic action has, at one time, been powerful in Queensland, especially in the northern districts; and along the coast pumice stone is met with in small pieces, brought, probably, by the tide. The great Coral Reef commences at Wide Bay, and continues to beyond Cape York; and much coarse coral is found even in Moreton Bay, which is largely used in place of lime in building.

## V.—CLIMATE.

But of what avail would be all this pasture-land, all this mineral-bearing rock, all this fertile soil, if there were not a climate to correspond,—if the penalty the white man must pay for the treasures of the country were to be certain disease and speedy death, or a prolonged life of physical prostration and misery? If the treasures of Queensland are not to be gathered except at such a price, better far that they should lie there for ever; and we, at least, would not write a line to induce any of Britain's sons to loosen their hold of the land of their birth for the purpose of going thither.

But the climate of Queensland is the very opposite of this. In the southern portion of the colony it is one of the finest in the world. For upwards of two years in succession, in all states of the weather, in all ways,—riding, working on the farm, studying under cover, speaking, boating, climbing hills, and crossing plains, felling trees, and burning timber, house building, and fruit planting,—I have tested it, and I am free to say that my measure of health during that period was equal to that enjoyed at home.

Many persons in this country have a very erroneous impression of the climate of North Australia; they fancy that the heat must be very great, and that the climate must be all but intolerable to the European constitution. Even in the older colonies this opinion prevailed to a great extent at one time; and although not entirely removed, yet it is now pretty generally admitted to be erroneous. I shall give an illustration of the false notion as it prevailed both here and there. In the year 1857, before leaving my native land, I met a friend one day on the street, who thus accosted me:—"So, you are going to Australia, I hear. What has put it into your head to go to such a place as Moreton Bay (Queensland)? You go to be roasted alive." I alleged that I had no great fondness for "par-boiling," and yet I was resolved to go thither. After three years' absence, two and a half of which were spent in this supposed salamandrine country, I met my friend again, neither shrivelled in bulk (I am fourteen stone) nor weakened in muscle, nor debilitated in any way. When passing through Sydney on my return home, some lady friends of mine (don't smile, I am a married man), whom I had met two and a half years before on my way north, expressed the greatest surprise to see me in robust health, and, with the utmost sincerity, inquired if Queensland was really not such a dreadfully hot country as it was represented to be? I assured them that what of health they saw to be in me I had brought direct from Queensland, as I had that evening arrived per steamer; that I liked the country much; that the climate was delicious, and that nothing but the most pressing necessity would or could have drawn me from it, even for a time. Much as I loved my dear old home, I was perfectly content with the country of my adoption.

This opinion is, doubtless, founded on the fact that the colony is situated partly without and partly within the tropic of Capricorn; but this conclusion is, nevertheless, arrived at in haste, and in forgetfulness, if not in ignorance, of another fact, namely, the modifying power that local causes imperceptibly but surely exert on climate. To judge of climate merely on the ground of distance from, or nearness to, the tropics, would lead, as it regards all countries so situated, to very erroneous conclusions; especially would this be the case in regard to Queensland. The same terms will not accurately describe the climate in all parts of such an immense country. There must, of necessity, be some difference in this respect between Cape York and Brisbane, between the Logan and the Leichhardt. Now, we have not data to fix the mean temperature of all these points, but we know, as a matter of fact, that white men live, labour, and are healthy, at Port Curtis, under the tropic of Capricorn; at Port Denison, 200 miles further north; on the Leichhardt Plains, and on the Maranoa and Darling Downs, as well as at Marybourgh and Brisbane. The mean temperature of the southern portion of the colony is ascertained with considerable accuracy, from observations taken by competent persons, over a period of several years, and the results which have been published in the colony, and which we will here reproduce, fully justify us in every remark we have made.

I was most desirous that the reader should have the advantage of my own experience and observation; but I am also anxious that he should have the benefit of the conclusions arrived at by other men. And that his confidence may have the firmer foundation, I shall quote only from the printed opinions of medical gentlemen who have been several years in the colony; and, as the question is one of prime importance to the emigrant, the extracts, though not long and heavy, will be full, and, I doubt not, to all reasonable minds, satisfactory.

The first is a letter, which is given entire, written by a medical gentleman, resident and practising in Rockhampton, just within the tropics, in answer to some remarks by a correspondent of the *Queensland Guardian*, the leading paper in the colony, and addressed to the editor. The date is June, 1860:—

"Sir,—I was very much surprised to find, in your issue of the 7th April, a letter signed 'Cotton,' wherein he states that a friend of his, who had recently returned overland from this place, describes the heat to be perfectly terrific, and that he was told by medical men that it would be quite impossible for Europeans to stand manual labour there in the mid-day heat: and that the origin of the prevalent diseases there could generally be traced to exposure to the sun, and that these were developing themselves in the offspring of these men, which was fast degenerating.

"The heat certainly was rather great during the summer months, but not so great as I have felt it either in South America or California, in which latter country persons from all parts of the world work during the heat; and in the course of four years' residence there, I only remember having seen one case of *coup de soleil*, and no disease brought on by exposure to the heat. I have been residing in this district for the last five years, and have not had (although the only medical practitioner, except at the time of the rush) any cases from exposure to the sun.

"I also can bear testimony that the offspring of the men who are so exposed, instead of degenerating, are as fine and healthy children as can be found in any portion of the continent of Australia, or even the whole world.

"If 'Cotton' would only pay us a visit just now, he would find the weather perfectly delicious, and quite cold enough. I have always found this district particularly healthy, the only epidemic being a mild form of influenza. I should feel obliged if 'Cotton's' friend would inform me what the prevalent diseases in this district are. 'Cotton's' friend must, I think, have received his information from some individuals who style themselves medical men, as from time to time a few such have made their appearance here. I am, &c.

"A. C. ROBERTSON, M.D., Surgeon."

A few years ago Dr. Hobbs, the health officer at Brisbane, discovered the curative qualities of the oil of the dugong fish; and, in a lecture on that new curative agent, which was published in the principal papers of the Australian colonies, he thus speaks of the climate of the southern portion of Queensland:—

"The discovery of such an agent within our own territory has long been considered a desideratum by the profession; and it does appear to be a remarkable as well as felicitous arrangement of nature, that, in a locality possessing, probably, one of the finest climates in the world,—combining both the soft, humid atmosphere of Torquay and Madeira in the summer, with the dry bracing air of Nice and Pau in the winter—the resort, too, of valetudinarians from all parts of the world,—a remedy should be found so potent in the treatment of chronic disorders."

In August of 1860, Dr. Barton, Meteorological Observer to the Government of Queensland, delivered a Lecture on Climate, from which we give an extract of great value. The length of it will be no bugbear to the reader who wishes to satisfy himself on this most important point:—

"I have now to consider the climate of this country, more particularly this colony, and principally this place (Brisbane). Humboldt divided the hemispheres each into six spaces or belts, from the knowledge that their temperature was nearly similar; the lines in the direction of, but not generally parallel to, the equator he called isothermal lines, and the spaces between them isothermal belts or zones. Thus in the northern hemisphere, London, New York, and Pekin are on the same—the fourth—isothermal line, their mean temperature approximating, though their climate and vegetable productions are very different. In the southern hemisphere, Queensland is in the second isothermal belt, which has a mean temperature of 68° to 77°. The Cape of Good Hope and Chili are in the same space. In the corresponding belt in the northern hemisphere are Funchal, in the island of Madeira, and Algiers, on the Mediterranean coast of Africa. The following results of temperature have been noted at those places:—

|  |  | Funchal. | Algiers. |
|---|---|---|---|
| Mean temperature of | warmest month | 75·5 | 82·8 |
| ,, | coldest months | 64·0 | 60·1 |
| ,, | year | 68·5 | 70·0 |
| ,, | winter | 64·4 | 61·5 |
| ,, | spring | 65·8 | 65·7 |
| ,, | summer | 72·5 | 80·2 |
| ,, | autumn | 72·3 | 72·5 |

"The contrast will here be seen between Algiers, a variable climate, and Funchal, an insular or constant one. It is very important to obtain the mean temperature as well as the extreme temperature of a place, as by these are climates classed as constant, variable, or extreme. Thus Funchal is constant, London and Paris variable, Pekin extreme; though the second and last, as I have just said, are on the same isothermal line. I am uncertain whether the climate of this neighbourhood should be classed amongst the constant or the variable: for although our temperature is generally very steady, yet the diurnal range is considerable, and at times very great; but on the whole I consider it entitled to be called a constant climate. We are indebted to the sea-breeze—tempering the heat of summer—for this equalization; it would not be felt further inland, and there greater variations of temperature might be expected. The climate of this colony, as well as of New South Wales, is salubrious, and very favourable to the European constitution: persons particularly who have arrived at, or passed, the middle age, in the more inhospitable climate of Britain, often have their health and vigour surprisingly renewed in this genial climate. Instances of persons arriving at great age are common,—persons nearly or quite one hundred years old being not unfrequently met with, and these generally retaining an amount of strength and activity to the last. From returns extending over many years of the diseases of troops in foreign stations, I find that while the rate of mortality in the Windward and Leeward Islands has been 92½ per 1,000 per annum, and in Jamaica 143 per 1,000, in Australia and the Cape of Good Hope the mean annual mortality has been at the minimum, or only 15 per 1,000. On this point Sir George Ballingall says of New South Wales, 'The climate generally is salubrious, although the heats in summer are excessive; the hottest and most unhealthy months are November, December, January, and February; the mean temperature during these months is 80 degrees; March and April may be looked upon as the rainy season.' The diseases occurring in Queensland from atmospheric causes, and most commonly noticed, are ague, continued fever, chronic rheumatism, and influenza; the first two being caused by the exhalation of vegetable miasm, the next by undue exposure to wet and night air, the last by some unknown state of the atmosphere, producing at first ordinary colds, which soon become infectious and epidemic. I will now make a few remarks on the results noted at this station (Brisbane) for a complete year, noticing each season separately; premising, however, that as the observations have only been taken for two or three years, the results may have to be modified somewhat, after the observations have extended over a number of years.

SPRING.—This season extends from September 23rd to December 22nd.

    Mean maximum heat of spring.............. 83·8
    Mean temperature ........................ 71·9
    Mean greatest diurnal range................ 33·9
    Mean diurnal range ...................... 25·3

SUMMER.—This season comprises the time between December 22nd and March 20th.

    Mean maximum heat of summer ............ 87·2
    Mean temperature ........................ 77·4
    Mean greatest diurnal range................ 30·1
    Mean diurnal range ...................... 20·4

AUTUMN.—Comprised between March 20th and June 24th.
  Mean maximum heat of autumn ............ 76·5
  Mean temperature ...................... 64·4
  Mean greatest diurnal range ............ 35·5
  Mean diurnal range .................... 23·6

WINTER.—Comprising the time between June 24th and September 23rd.
  Mean maximum heat of winter ............ 75·0
  Mean temperature ...................... 61·1
  Mean greatest diurnal range ............ 39·2
  Mean diurnal range .................... 27·2

  Mean maximum heat of year.............. 80·6
  Mean temperature of year .............. 68·7
  Mean greatest diurnal range ............ 31·7
  Mean diurnal range .................... 24·1

"The temperature of the year, then, as thus carefully ascertained, we see is 68·7, almost exactly the same as that of Funchal, in the island of Madeira, which we have seen to be 68·5, and which place, as already stated, is in the corresponding isothermal belt of the northern hemisphere, being classed amongst the insular or constant climates, and of world-wide repute for the salubrity of its climate. But while I unexpectedly find this almost exact coincidence of mean temperature between Brisbane and Funchal, still I must notice that the range of temperature, both in summer and winter, is several degrees greater here than in Madeira, the summer here being a little hotter, and the winter colder."

The following table, compiled from the most reliable data, gives the mean annual temperature, average fall of rain in inches, and average number of days on which rain fell at seven points, far apart from each other:—

| Places. | Latitude. | Mean annual temperature. | Average rain fall in inches. | Average number of days on which rain fell. |
|---|---|---|---|---|
| Brisbane (Queensland) ... | 28° S. | 68·7 | 43 | 108 |
| Funchal (Madeira)......... | 32° 37′ N. | 68·5 | 29 | 70 |
| Cape Town ............... | 34° S. | 67 | 29 | 76 |
| Malta ................... | 35° 53′ N. | 67 | 28 | 75 |
| Algiers .................. | 36° N. | 70 | 36 | 75 |
| Mauritius................ | 20° 9′ S. | 77 | 39 | 148 |
| London................... | 51° 30′ N. | 50·4 | 23 | 148 |

The abundance of rain that falls in Queensland is distributed over a number of days, 108 in the 365, and a large portion falls in the hot months, which secures the grazers and farmers against the continuous droughts that are so injurious in the south; and from the physical features of the country, and the nature of the prevailing soil, the temperature is cool for the latitude, and the atmosphere pure, dry, and buoyant. The "hot winds" and "brick-fielders," that at times sweep across the southern colonies, or visit localities where the soil is sandy and loose, withering every green thing, and overwhelming both man and beast in terrible prostration, are unknown in Queensland. Occasionally the west winds are dry and parching, but never to the extent of being seriously injurious to vegetation. All along the coast the never-failing sea breeze, springing up about ten in the morning and continuing till four P.M., moderates the powerful heat of the sun; whilst in the interior, where the country is open, and where the sea breeze rarely penetrates, the average temperature is sensibly lower. Perhaps in no warm country in the world can the European constitution stand a greater amount of heat with impunity than in this. Extremes are not so great, or not so sensibly felt, transitions are not so rapid, or not so injurious, as in most other warm climes; and hence Queensland is the resort of invalids from New Zealand, Tasmania, Victoria, New South Wales, and India. I have known gentlemen from all these countries, and from Scotland and England too, come to Queensland in search of health; and whilst many had been too late in coming, others found the precious boon, and returned to their respective posts again. Speaking of consumptive cases, Dr. Hobbs writes:—"Many persons afflicted with this fatal malady have derived great benefit from a short residence in Queensland; and several persons who have arrived in what appeared to be a dying state have lived here for years in comparative health and comfort."

In a document, issued under the sanction and by the authority of the Government of the colony, the following remarks occur:—"During a large proportion of the year the weather is fine, the sky cloudless, the atmosphere dry, elastic, and exhilarating. The summer months (December, January, and February) are hot, but not sultry, or oppressive. The winter season, when dry, which it almost always is, is exceedingly beautiful and agreeable. The mornings and evenings are cool; during the day the air is warm and balmy, the sky brilliantly blue, and the atmosphere singularly transparent. Such a climate is necessarily healthy. It is free from all endemic diseases, and epidemics are of rare occurence. The diseases incidental to youth are usually very mild in their character, and short in their duration."

Let no one be deceived. Disease walks about there as here, notwithstanding the admirable climate with which the colony is blessed. Men grow old and feeble in the course of years, and go down to the dust in that country as well as in this; but much of the disease is brought on and perpetuated by men's own thoughtlessness and folly. Strong drink is a terrible colonial scourge, and he does his work there in double quick time. High wages enable the working man to have his rum, his gin, or his brandy, if he is so inclined; and when he abandons himself to the fiery cup, a double infatuation appears to seize him, and, heedless of all warning and all consequences, he rushes onwards to certain and often sudden death. In the Australian colonies, the verdict which the newspapers carry over the world,—" Death by sun-stroke," should often be " Death by brandy."

The sum of the whole is this:—The climate of Queensland, though warm, is remarkably healthy; and in the case of those Europeans who combine care with industry, sobriety with high wages, it is productive of a fair share of physical enjoyment, and is not inimical to longevity.

## VI.—MOTIVES TO EMIGRATION.

The statements contained in the previous chapters may be considered as sufficient to convince the candid reader that Queensland is a magnificent pastoral country, and that the climate, upon the whole, is so genial and so healthy, that pastoral pursuits may be carried on there with maximum advantages and minimum drawbacks. In certain portions of the colony, cattle and horses are the most suitable stock; in other and larger portions, sheep constitute the stock most valuable to the grazing farmer; but in all parts, with the exception of here and there, a patch of sandy plain, or occasionally flooded ground, or rough, scraggy quartzy ridges, such as those to the north-west of Brisbane, the vegetation, suited to the support of the finest herds and flocks, exists in the greatest abundance. Rarely is there a continuous drought in Queensland, although, of course, some seasons the feed is not so good as it is in others. The seasons vary there as elsewhere, but the variations are neither so marked, nor so damaging, as in many other countries. It is not necessary that the land should be all rich, that the climate should be faultless, that neither sheep nor men should become diseased, in order that the claims of such a country should be established. The man of common sense and observation will see at a glance, that in balancing the claims of countries, as regards their pastoral capabilities, Queensland will not stand at the bottom of the list.

But, after all, "the proof of the pudding is in the eating of it." We might be able to show that all the known conditions of a pastoral country meet in the new colony, and yet, from conditions not cognizable by us, it might result that neither sheep nor cattle throve there. There might be something in the grasses, in the soils, or in the climate, that might be injurious to the health and prosperity of imported stock. But this is proved not to be the case in Queensland, by the most satisfactory of all processes—experiment. Millions of sheep and thousands of cattle and horses are, at this moment, depasturing in that country in the finest condition, and with highly satisfactory results to the proprietors. The conditions of success are within the reach of every man who gives himself to that department of colonial enterprise, and who brings to it a reasonable capital, and ordinary attention and management. These are, that he select a good run, fairly grassed and watered, and put on it stock young and healthy.

Squatting is a colonial term equivalent to the English term pastoral, only the scale on which pastoral operations are carried on in the Australian colonies is very large. The "runs" of the Australian squatters are vast in comparison with the largest sheep-farms in Britain; and though their flocks may not be proportionably large, yet they far outnumber those of their home compeers. The profits, too, exceed those of the home sheep-farmer; the one may be counted in thousands, while the other rarely rises above hundreds.

Squatter was at one time a term of reproach, but now it designates a peculiar class, held in honourable estimation by the body of colonists. It is representative of a class of men without whom the Australian colonies could not prosper. This term is in use in America as well as in Australia, but with a different signification. In the former country it generally designates the sturdy and daring backwoodsman, who selects, at will, a portion of wild bush on which he "squats," that is, settles himself and family in an easy way, which he improves after his own notions, and which he has the opportunity of securing as his own, when the land comes to be disposed of by Government. In Australia it always designates a class of men who hold, many of them, hundreds of thousands of acres of land at a nominal rent; possess immense flocks and herds; draw large revenues from their stations or runs; have a tendency to become non-resident; and who constitute the peculiar aristocracy of the colonies.

The aristocracy of the southern hemisphere is not pure or select, and it has not a "long pedigree," but neither is it "penniless." It is rather a heterogeneous mass of recent conglomeration, and yet a mass in which there is much vitality. In it you will find the younger sons of noble families, adventurous members of commercial houses, cautious Scotch and English farmers, members of the bar, sons of the church, and men who have risen from nearly all the classes of honourable industry. Varied though their tastes may be, diverse though their characters are, gathered from all grades of society though they have been, yet the squatting fraternity have many important interests in common, and constitute a very powerful party in the country.

I have been brought into contact with many individuals belonging to this class in Queensland and in New South Wales, both in a private and public capacity, and I am bound to say, that, as a class, I found them to be highly honourable men. The first Parliament of Queensland, which has acquitted itself so well, which has put on the Statute Book of the colony laws that do them immortal honour, and that have laid the bases of great national prosperity, was largely composed of squatters.

Among this class in Queensland, you will find many men of cultivated tastes, large mental endowments and attainments, unimpeachable rectitude, and large generosity. They are proverbial for their hospitality, and no traveller in the bush is ever at a loss should he strike a track that leads to a station.

But, as a matter of course, there are to be found among them men of a very different stamp,—selfish, despotic, unjust, cruel, untruthful, proud, licentious, with whom no man can make out his service, and no woman can retain her virtue. But these cases are now rare, a very marked improvement having taken place within the last few years. I have met with squatters whose education was defective, whose manner of doing business was "smart," who were reported hard masters, but I have only once seen a member of the fraternity who, to a head empty as an exhausted receiver, added a step, and look, and growl like some pigmy Jupiter.

For a long while the squatting interest has scarcely come up before the mind of the home public, owing to the sound and fury of the gold-gathering mania, and owing partly to the fact, that those connected with it have, to a remarkable degree, by nature or by training, mastered the admirable art of remaining silent. In colonies generally the people are very communicative; they will blurt out everything; nothing seems to delight them more than "bounce;" but you will not find squatters saying much about themselves, except it be to protest against some apparent or real encroachment on their interests or privileges. They content themselves in silence, with the steady increase of their flocks, the unfailing demand for their wool, and the plenty with which their table is spread. In some quarters, the condition of the squatter is not so satisfactory, but in Queensland he could scarcely muster a grievance, and it would be unreasonable to expect that he should tell all the world of his prosperity. Influenced by no hostile feeling to the squatters, or any other class in the colony, but by an honest determination to describe accurately its character, and to enumerate faithfully its great resources, I set myself to tell the truth so far as I know it, both as it regards the squatter and the farmer. In this way I shall the better serve the interests of the colony at large, and have the opportunity of placing before the men of various tastes and of different pursuits in this country, the numerous attractions that point to the improvement of their material circumstances, were they to emigrate to this good land.

Gold is a powerful—the most powerful—motive to take men across the seas; but if we were really to look to the actual state of things, we should see that there are other motives, under whose influence, if a man may not always become so speedily rich, it is much more safe for him to place himself. Many gold-fields are illusory: much more is sunk in them than extracted from them. Besides, the richest gold-claim becomes exhausted, and not unfrequently wastes the life of him who works it. There is not one gold-digger in fifty successful, as men are reckoned successful in Australia. The average wage of the gold-digger is below the wage of the industrious artizan. This has been proved by the statistical returns in Victoria. There are, indeed, fortunate individuals. In a year or two they amass a competency, and retire to spend their days in quiet comfort; or they continue, and sink it all in some new but hungry claim. You hear of the wonderful gain; you do not hear of the sudden loss. You have held up to your astonished gaze, in all public papers, the man who has got his "nugget" of many ounces; but nothing is said of the thousands with their empty purses, haggard looks, and broken constitutions, who form the contrast to this great virtual deception.

I have questioned many men who have tried their hand at the diggings, and, in most instances, they frankly acknowledged that, in point of money, they were nothing the better for the attempt, but, in the matter of experience, had gained much. Others I have met, who had been successful; but, in several instances, just as they had secured a fortune or a competency, and thought about retiring from the crushing work of the mine, a monitor, whose voice could not any longer be hushed, insisted that, in a very different sense, their "house should be put in order," and preparations made for the journey which is performed "without scrip, or staff, or purse," to that bourne from which no mortal ever returns.

I well remember a case that greatly interested me, and which illustrates this point with painful particularity. For some time after I reached the colony, and before a church was erected for my use, I was constrained to conduct divine service in the large hall of the School of Arts, Brisbane. In the state of the colony, the steamer bringing every week a score or two strangers from the older colonies, many strange faces appeared in the hall. But one day my eye was arrested, and my sympathy awakened, by an interesting young man who came in late, and almost stealthily took his seat near the door. Others observed him besides the speaker, but no one seemed to know anything about him. Sunday after Sunday he made his appearance, always late, always with a soft step, always took his seat near the door, and moved away immediately when the benediction was pronounced. He seemed a stranger in that strange land, and yet he had found his way to the "place where prayer was wont to be made." I could see he was much interested in the theme of discourse, and sometimes moved to tears. He appeared to be in very bad health.

By and bye his attendance was not so regular, and now it was that I learned his name and residence. He was a young gentleman from Victoria, who had sought, in the genial climate of Queensland, respite, if not deliverance, from that relentless enemy of so many of our young men and women—consumption. The disease was very far gone, and its progress was too rapid to leave a doubt on the mind what would be the result. He was too late, as he told me afterwards, in coming to Queensland: even the genial air of that clime could now do him little good.

When he could no longer come, or come but at intervals, to the public worship of God, he preferred a polite request that I should pay him a visit in his lodgings. Of course, I did so, and continued to do so till his death.

The substance of what I learned was this, and I am guilty of no breach of confidence in thus referring to the case, for on several occasions he expressed an anxious desire that young men who might come to know of his career and its premature close might learn the sad lesson it was well calculated to teach. He was the son of English parents, who were now dead, had been well educated and carefully brought up; in the time of the gold mania, like many other young men, he had left the desk of the clerk for the spade and pick of the digger. He found it much harder work than he anticipated, but was determined to go forward. What he had not the physical power to do, he determined to accomplish by tact. He selected for his mates (there were four of them altogether) as powerful men as he could find, and, by his intelligence, urbanity, and lively humour, succeeded in keeping them in excellent spirits. "Here I was," he said, "dooming myself to the society of men coarse and often unfeeling, all for the love of gold. Fool that I was! I have got it; but oh, what have I lost! I know that I have sacrificed my life."

It was true. By exposing himself to the many discomforts of the gold-digger's life for several years, he had completely destroyed his constitution, and just when he had realized a competency he retired—to die. His Bible was his constant companion from the time that I knew him, and though far from friends, the voice and the hand of Christian sympathy soothed his last moments, and performed the last services. Peace to his ashes! but let not the lesson of his life be lost.

I am not to be supposed as writing against mining for gold and other metals as an important department of colonial enterprize, but simply as lifting a warning voice against the heedless rush that is sometimes made in that direction, and making some attempt to show that there are other motives besides the gold mines that should have a favourable influence on our plans regarding the future. There are gold-fields in Queensland as well as in the other colonies, and these will be worked some day; but meanwhile there are other sources of wealth and comfort open to British capital and skill, and which will yield a more certain and a more equally distributed return. To these we would specially direct the attention of industrious working men, and men with small capital.

Farming is in its infancy in Queensland, and of the 37,000 inhabitants which, at the moment we write, may be scattered over the southern portion of the colony, a small proportion are engaged in agricultural pursuits. Yet we do not doubt that we shall succeed in proving to the candid reader, that in this department of colonial enterprise, as well as in the pastoral, there is a boundless field for the successful application of British labour, skill, and capital. While large capitalists will look towards the squatting interest for the profitable employment of their money, or to mercantile pursuits, or to the cultivation of cotton, sugar, &c., on a large scale, the men of small means, and the men whose capital is their labour, will naturally look towards the cultivation of the soil in the production of all those articles of necessity or of luxury which a prosperous community requires, and a warm climate renders indispensable. And there is room for any number of the industrious workmen, who may have the utmost difficulty in gaining a reasonable remuneration for their labour here, on the large and fertile agricultural reserves that lie, one might say, ready for cultivation in Queensland, and offering to the cultivator a reward amply remunerative for all his self-sacrifice and toil. Few things would be more conducive to the real and permanent prosperity of the colony than a large influx of industrious working men with their families; and no where in the world is there open, at this moment, a field more attractive, and more certainly productive of material results, to men whose honour it is that they obtain their honest "bread by the sweat of the brow." The hand of the willing need never be idle there, and many are the ways in which a living may be made; but we would strongly counsel that most emigrants who will certainly leave these shores for the new colony should betake themselves to the land. Other things may promise a larger and a more speedy return; but don't be in too great haste to get rich. Nothing is surer than the soil; and its products in the shape of grain, and roots, and fruits for colonial consumption, and in the shape of cotton, and it may be sugar, and various other articles for the supply of the home market, will never be out of demand.

Most men in leaving their native land, in braving the dangers of the sea, and in quietly submitting to the necessary changes and difficulties that beset one when they first commence operations in a new and strange country, are actuated by the laudable and natural desire of bettering their worldly circumstances, or of placing their families in a position whence they may, by industry and perseverance, command for themselves honourable and lasting success. Various are the motives by which men are moved to emigrate—various are the courses which they will pursue; but, in adopting Queensland as your home, it is immaterial on which department of enterprise you determine to enter, provided your choice corresponds with your capital, and your colonial life is characterized by honourable activity.

## VII.—SQUATTING.

Squatting is an ancient and honourable occupation, and in ordinary circumstances is not one of the least lucrative. The nomade life of the Arab, and that of the Jewish patriarchs of the old time, are alike developments of this primeval mode of providing for one's family, and accumulating wealth. Nothing could be more natural; it is the development of a great law— the law of increase. The head of the family is in possession of a few goats, or camels, or sheep, or oxen, or asses, and these go on increasing, thus providing the household with milk, and meat, and clothing, and labour, and adding annually to the wealth, and position, and importance of the patriarch. In a few years Abraham and Jacob, from being shepherds with slender means, and of little social importance, grew up, under the blessing of Heaven, to be squatters with enormous flocks and herds, whose proximity disturbed large tribes, and whose wealth raised envy in the breast of kings.

There are, however, points of difference as well as points of coincidence. The patriarch of old moved from district to district according to the condition of the grass, the water, and the season; the colonial squatter has his run, always ample enough for his flocks, fixed by the rules that regulate civilized communities, and he must take his chance of the seasons. The patriarch grazed his flocks free over the rich valleys and well-watered plains, included within the bounds of his uncontrolled wanderings; our squatter must pay a sum to the Government in the shape of rent and assessment—small, indeed, in comparison with his annual profits, for the opportunity of depasturing his cattle and sheep on certain defined lands, and for the protection to himself and property, which the Government affords. The patriarch reckoned the increase of his stock the great source of profit, the wool, and hides, and tallow, and horns, and bones, going for little; the modern squatter manages to make the "clip" of his flocks pay the expenses of his station, and these are considerably heavier, we may suppose, than those of an ancient patriarchal household, while his profits are derived from the increase (minimum 50 per cent.) with the addition of other items that advanced civilization has rendered of some value. The patriarchs seem to have had, sometimes at least, town or village houses, but when on their wandering and grazing expeditions, they lived in tents with their servants; your full-blown squatter has his town house in Melbourne, Sydney, or Brisbane, perhaps some snug little estate in old England to boot; and on the run itself a substantial hard-wood dwelling and offices, of ample dimensions, and supplied with comforts and even luxuries that you would scarcely expect to meet with in the wild bush. Favourable as were the circumstances in which many of the patriarchs were placed, and rapid as was the growth of their flocks and herds, the position and the profits of the modern squatter, with a well-selected, well-stocked run, are greatly to be preferred.

Like the heads of households in ancient times, the squatter is hospitable, generous, and frequently entertains strangers. His house is sometimes, indeed, the only place where a traveller can find shelter for himself within a circuit of many miles; and masters and managers are alike in this matter. All welcome the passers by, give what shelter they have, and wish them good speed in the morning.

In connexion with squatting and bush life generally, I have often met with beautiful illustrations of ancient usages mentioned in the Holy Scriptures. The "wells" that the patriarchs are represented as digging, and for which rival herdsmen occasionally strove, have their counter-parts in the "water-holes" that every squatter knows to be indispensable to a good run, and which every purchaser of only a few acres secures to his farm if he possibly can. Many a time I have heard the inquiry, when some one had made a purchase,—"Has it got a water-hole?" Indeed, this is generally the first question which a knowing hand puts to the purchaser. And in such a climate as that of Queensland, water is an indispensable article. Never purchase land unless there is water supply upon it, or an easy approach to some government water reserve. Government exercises a sort of paternal care over small proprietors in this matter, and consequently, in all directions, there are fresh-water reserves for the general good, and thus no one is at liberty to monopolise an element of such prime importance.

Whether a "kid of the goats," or a "lamb of the flock," may not sometimes be offered literally to the stranger, I cannot myself positively affirm, but that "the hen that sits nearest the cock" is sometimes so served up, I know to be a fact. Never have I met with more genuine and unostentatious hospitality and kindness than in the Australian bush. There, too, you will witness baking according to the primeval mode. "Cakes baked on the hearth," composed of flour and water, are very common fare in the bush, although on stations the process is more civilized. The American camp oven is very handy, and is coming into general use all over the country, where, as yet, neither baker nor butcher plies his trade. A man must be his own butcher, and a housewife her own baker; and where men herd together or live alone without the softening and elevating influence of virtuous woman, they must be both their own butcher and baker.

The baking process is very simple. Outside the wooden hut, or "humpy," as the black fellows name it, a level spot is selected on which to have the fire needed only for cooking purposes; over the spot there is sometimes a frail canopy of bark placed to shelter the cook from the sun, or perchance, which is more probable, to prevent the thunder-storms from extinguishing the fire, or the rain from spoiling the batch or the broth. The fire-place consists of two or three flat stones placed together like rude pavement, and on these the fuel is placed; when the stones have been sufficiently heated, the embers are brushed aside, and the cakes are placed on them. The embers, still in a glow, are then spread over the cakes, and in a short time out comes the far-famed Australian "damper," fit for immediate use. There are worse things than "salt beef and damper," I can tell you, when one has worked all day with the saw, the axe, or the spade, or when one has dismounted after a long day's solitary journey. The food is perfectly wholesome, and yields substantial support to the brawny arm of the bushman; and even he who is town-bred, and accustomed to town living, finds little difficulty in digesting it in the circumstances alluded to. I have dined as heartily on beef and damper in the humpy of a little settler in the Australian bush as ever I did on the roast beef of old England. Everything wholesome is good when one is hungry, and few things contribute more certainly to a good appetite than a stiff day's work in the bush; and there, no well-doing man need ever suffer from the pangs of hunger. Industry brings enough and to spare for both man and beast.

Millions of acres, as we have seen, are open to the squatter in Queensland. He must go into the far interior, and leave the lands by the sea and the navigable rivers to the farmer and cotton grower. The squatter is the pioneer of a new country. He not only introduces sheep, cattle, and horses into the country, but he thereby vastly improves the pasture lands. Grasses become more sweet and actually become more numerous by grazing. The interests of this class, therefore, should not be overlooked in the legislature of a colony: they are also the pioneers of population as well as of stock. Around the station there spring up in a short time the huts of shepherds and stock men; and these, again, soon become the nucleus of little clumps of dwellings,—woodmen, bullock-drivers, carpenters, horse-breakers, tailors, shoemakers, and such like, gradually congregate, till, on some large stations, the population becomes considerable. At the resting-places of the drays that "do the carrying" to and from the stations, there rise the way-side inn and smith's forge; and these in time become miniature villages, where dogs, and cows, and children vie with each other in numbers, and all alike revel in wild freedom. This is one way in which population spreads, and finds its home hundreds of miles from the large and populous towns. The governmental method is to lay out townships in various directions, have the surrounding lands surveyed, and encourage suitable persons to purchase, and take up their abode in these localities.

The country for many miles beyond the centres of population is occupied with stock, so that the squatter is compelled to push further and further to the west and north. The low lying districts are more favourable for cattle than for sheep; and horses are reared anywhere, although all breeds are not alike valuable. The lands on the Logan, the Brisbane, the Mary, the Burnett, the Fitzroy, the Condamine, the Dawson, are all taken up, and partially if not wholly stocked; and these include a vast expanse of country. The flow of the great squatting enterprise is now towards the Malonne, the Mackenzie, the Isaacs, the Comet, and the Burdekin, the outlying rivers of this magnificent country. And when these are appropriated, as they very soon will be, the daring and enterprise of the pioneer squatter will carry him forwards, still west and north, till he shall feed his flocks on those well-watered plains from which Stuart was driven by the hostile blacks.

The squatting system is of vast extent and of vast importance, but in neither is it expanded in Queensland to anything like its proper dimensions. These are measured only by the extent of its acres and the richness of its pastures. In this new colony there is, even in regard to the pastoral interest—the interest that is first developed—much land to be possessed; for not only is there a large outlying country, on which not a single head of cattle or sheep is yet to be seen, beyond the farthest stations at present occupied, but none of the stations that have been in operation for years are stocked to anything like the amount they are capable of sustaining. The flow of men and capital to Queensland from the other Australian colonies, with the view of engaging in the squatting enterprise under the liberal and just laws that the first Legislature of the colony enacted, may almost be called "a rush;" and this fact, to which the Melbourne and Sydney papers, as well as those of Brisbane, bear constant and increasing testimony, is the strongest proof that could be presented in favour of the pastoral enterprise in Queensland. Men who have been for years connected with mercantile, agricultural, and pastoral pursuits in Victoria, Tasmania, New Zealand, and New South Wales, are not at all likely to invest their capital and to take up their abode in the north unless they are assured that the pasture is good and abundant, and that the laws of the colony are liberal and just. These men know what they are about. But I would that emigrants were to go direct to Queensland, and not in this roundabout way. By going direct and at once, whatever may be your ulterior intentions, your chances are greater, and you secure the liberal advantages held out by the Government. By first going to other colonies, and then making your way from Melbourne or Sydney to Brisbane, you first lose time, and then place yourselves beyond the free grants of land. But this shall be fully explained under the proper head.

## VIII.—HOW TO SECURE A "RUN."

Although the major part of the readers of this little work who resolve to emigrate to Queensland may do so in connexion with agricultural pursuits, yet some of them may have both the taste and the capital to justify them in turning their attention to the squatting department. For their sakes especially, but also for the information of all parties, I shall now tell how a person may secure to himself a Run, and with what capital he may commence with the reasonable prospect of success.

I am concerned to create a true interest in the colony. Every statement is in accordance with the acts of the Colonial Parliament, discussed and enacted during my residence there, and copies of which are now on my table; but I shall not increase the size and price of this volume by transcribing these documents, or even quoting largely from them. I was present in the House of Assembly when most of the land laws of Queensland were discussed, and in their printed form, as assented to by His Excellency the Governor, I have carefully studied them in my home retreat; and shall, therefore, place before the reader the most accurate information in the most condensed and popular form I can.

You have got a capital of £750, and on this you cannot manage, with the utmost care and economy, to raise annually more than the merest necessaries of life. You have nothing to meet contingencies; you can lay by nothing for "a rainy day." It is hard for you, an industrious man with a wife and family, to waste the best portion of your days, and all your young and buoyant energies, in simply procuring bread. You have a right to expect, under a benign Providence, that such a capital should realize something against the decline of life. You love your native land; "breathes there a man with soul so dead," that he does not? But the claims of your family are paramount, and you resolve to emigrate to Queensland. You don't go alone, for several of your neighbours, worse or better off, have taken the same resolution.

The sea is crossed, and you have set foot on land. Your money is secure in the bank, and you have received the "land orders" for the passage-money which you paid for yourself, wife, and family. Everything is strange, and yet everything looks uncommonly English. You look about; you select your "free grants" of land; you find that things are not so strange after all. You take some light work; perhaps you engage yourself to a sheep station for six or twelve months. Your wife and family stay in Brisbane.

What! take a day's work, play the shepherd on another man's station, and £750 placed to your credit in the bank; Why not, friend? Are you above that? Then, think no more of emigrating. This is the way to gain colonial experience without encroaching on your capital; and experience is of vast importance in every colony. Experience may enable you to realize a fortune out of your small capital; proceed without this help, and your capital may—very likely will—become "small by degrees, and beautifully less."

But you have gained the necessary experience, how or where it concerns no one to know; and you desire to settle on a run, or sheep-farm. You have ascertained by this time that there are Commissioners appointed by the Governor and Executive Council for the different squatting districts, whose duty it is to attend to all applications for new runs, when made in proper form, and to give information to those who know not how to apply.

The run may be selected anywhere you like, outside of those already appropriated, in accordance with reasonable conditions, regarding your neighbour's boundaries, water frontage, &c. You ride over the portion of land you fancy, accompanied by a friend, or an agent, and mark its boundaries by notching prominent trees, or running your lines by creeks, or dry channels, or mountain spurs. You must see that it lies as compact as possible; for Government will not allow the pasture lands to be cut up in a wasteful manner. Starting from the furthest boundary of your neighbour's run, you thus, with the help of your friend, lay out a block of land of twenty-five square miles, and you carry in your hand a simple outline of the run, accompanied by a few sentences of a descriptive or explanatory nature, to the District Commissioner. He receives you with the utmost civility; enters your application and the descriptive sentences in his large book; and even corrects your description should it be incorrect, as he knows much more about the district than you do yet. If the land is not pre-occupied—of course, this is ascertained before you lodge your application, —and if you are the first applicant, the Commissioner grants a *license* for you to occupy the run for *one year*.

This book is open to the public, and, on the payment of a fee of 2s. 6d., any one may examine it, to ascertain what runs are taken up, and by whom. But, in order that everything may be done openly and without favour, all applications are from time to time published in the *Queensland Gazette*.

No run is to contain less than 25 square miles, and none are to contain more than 100; but one man may take as many runs as he likes, provided always that he complies with the terms of lease, which are framed to suit the *bonâ fide* squatter, and not the speculator; for in colonies men speculate in everything, even in runs, to the extensive detriment of the pastoral interest. I have supposed that you have selected one of 25 square miles. The estimated capability of this run is 100 sheep for each square mile, or 20 head of cattle, should it be taken as a cattle station.

The license is now obtained from the District Commissioner, and within 90 day from the signing of that document you are required to pay, as an occupation fee for the year, the sum of 10s. per square mile; and unless such fee be paid, the license is forfeited to the crown. You may put as many sheep on your run the first year as you like; and the occupation fee, £12 10s., constitutes, in fact, the rent for the year.

It is very probable that when you have had a six months' trial of your block of land of 25 square miles, for which you pay the Government £12 10s., you would like to secure it on *lease*. How are you then to proceed in order to accomplish your object? Any time during the year of license, three clear months before the license expires, you may make application to the Chief Commissioner of Crown Lands, through the District Commissioner, for a lease; and should you comply with the terms, and the way be clear, a lease for 14 years will be granted. The way is clear if there is no rival applicant (priority settles the claim), and should the land not be required for public purposes, such as townships, agricultural reserves, &c.

There is one reasonable condition, and it is faithfully carried out: during the year of license, and at the date of the application for the lease, you must have your 25 square mile block stocked to an extent equal to one-fourth of the number of sheep, or equivalent number of cattle, which it is deemed capable of carrying by the Act. The Government estimate is, that your 25 square miles will carry 2,500 sheep—in reality, it will carry a much greater number, but the Government does not wish to be too exacting with its children, and the number, therefore, which must be depasturing on it when the application is forwarded, is 625. Six hundred good sheep may be bought at the present time for less than £500. This is the condition which has been inserted in the Queensland Squatting Law, to curb, if it may not prevent, speculation.

The District Commissioner grants you the license for one year. On your application, the license is converted into a 14 years' lease, on the condition mentioned, by the Chief Commissioner of Crown Lands.

When the lease has been secured, what is the rent you will require to pay for your 25 square miles? Just the same for the first four years as you paid the year of license, £12 10s. And suppose you have on the run 2,500 sheep, then the annual rent you pay per sheep is 1¼d. ! And, to use the words of the Act, "the rent payable in respect of such lease for the succeeding periods of five years and five years, being the residue of the term comprised in such lease, shall be the appraisement at the commencement of such periods of five years and five years respectively, in proportion to the value of the run, its capabilities, advantages, and disadvantages being considered." But it is provided by the Act, that in no case during the first period of five years shall the rent be less than £25, or greater than £50, per block of 25 square miles. During the last five years of the lease, the same sized run will not pay less than £30, and not more than £70. This is deemed very fair, as the value of runs greatly increases from various causes during the period of 14 years.

Should any difference arise between the squatter and the Government, it is settled by arbitration; and should the lessee pay his rent regularly, and the land not be required for public purposes, he sits unmolested, absolute "monarch of all he surveys." He has no wild beasts to contend with, and if he has the good sense and the humanity to take the poor wandering blacks on the right side, they will prove as harmless to him and his, as is the timid walleby or kangaroo. Should your little principality be required for Governmental or public purposes, you have a twelvemonths' warning to quit, and compensation for all the improvements, such as house, huts, offices, stock-yard, and wells.

I have kept close to the Acts of the Assembly in the above sketch, without fatiguing the reader with the formal and ponderous clauses of the Acts themselves. Provision is made for the passage of stock from district to district, when runs are being changed, or new ones occupied. No one is at liberty to occupy any run, however far off it may be, without a license in the first instance, and then a lease; and defaulters are smartly called to account. The greatest precaution is used, under the authority of Act of the Assembly, to preserve the healthy flocks from the diseased. There is very little disease, indeed, among the Queensland flocks, but as sheep may be seized with scab, influenza, &c., less precaution would be culpable. In all the Australian colonies, the law is stringent on this point, and judging from the past, we may believe not without sufficient reason. It is not only that the sheep that mingle with the diseased flocks shall catch the contagion, but even the ground on which the diseased flock feeds receives it, and a long time after will infect a perfectly healthy flock that may be placed on the run.*

You see what you can do with your little capital of £750, were you disposed to turn squatter.

## IX.—SQUATTING AND BRITISH LABOUR.

There may be at this date about 500 squatters in Queensland, occupying stations of various dimensions, none of them smaller than 25 square miles. According to the law of the new colony, every station must have its proportion of stock. A certain

---

\* The reader is referred to
An Act for Regulating the Occupation of Unoccupied Crown Lands in the Unsettled Districts;
An Act to Regulate the Occupation of Land applied for by Tender; and
An Act to Provide for the Leasing of Crown Lands previously occupied.
The date on which these Acts received the assent of the Governor was 17th September, 1860.

amount of labour, therefore, is necessary for the profitable carrying on of the stations. No runs in Queensland are now allowed to lie waste, waiting till the lessee should meet with a rich goose to whom he might sell it for a "consideration," to the tune of one or two thousand pounds. That state of matters is passed. The run that is not stocked to the extent of one-fourth of its estimated capabilities is, as we have seen, forfeited to the Crown, and immediately let to one who shall observe the terms of occupation.

The number of stations, therefore, represents a certain amount of labour, although, from the absence of statistics, we are unable to give the proportions. And as the number is steadily, and even rapidly increasing every year, and as the labour on each station increases annually with the increase of the stock, the demand for labour in the squatting department must be greater and greater year by year. But, in addition to this, every year sees many men who have saved £50 or £100 as shepherds or stockmen return to the towns, in the neighbourhoods of which they purchase small farms, and settle down into cultivators of the soil. The squatter, therefore, has a constant demand for labour, and this demand increases year by year. All classes of men may engage in this work; and, in point of fact, you will at this moment find men busy at station work, representatives of all grades in English society. It is in some sense a "Refuge," for there you will meet decayed members of the learned professions, sprigs of nobility, too "fast" for home society, doing their part alongside of the shepherd from the Cheviots, and the ploughman from Lothian and Essex, and doing it well; for, keep them from the gin and the brandy bottle, and they make very fair shepherds and stockmen. Few will surpass them in working a dog with sheep, or tracking, on the fleetest horse on the station, a mob of cattle or horses. But after all, the men the squatter likes best to have about him are those who, at home, were accustomed to out-door work. There is very little Chinese or coolie labour employed on stations, for, though considerably cheaper than British labour, it is by no means so efficient. Besides, as yet there are few coolies in Queensland, and the Chinese prefer following in the wake of the British gold-digger. So far as I have had the opportunity of judging, the gold-fields attract John Chinaman to Australia, and when there, he has no difficulty in showing that he has little liking for any other work. I am speaking of the present state of things: were the Chinese to be introduced to cultivate the soil, it might turn out otherwise. Germans are employed in considerable numbers in connexion with stations, and make as a rule good servants. They are sober, industrious, and plodding, and on good terms with the British emigrants.

Our opinion, therefore, is, that the labour which the squatter will continue to employ, should the working-men go out in sufficient numbers to keep up the supply, is that which Britain alone can provide from her surplus population.

Some reader will say, "So far, well; but, before we can think seriously of emigrating, we should like to know somewhat of the labour that is expected of a man on the great sheep-farms of Queensland. We know what is what, pretty much, in the present, and we should like to know what is before us, were we to pack up and go. Nay, we must know this *before* we resolve."

Right, my friend; you are just the man for the colony. Keep your eyes open; take nothing for granted; but when the proof is before you of the goodness of the land, do not hesitate to act.

When the station is small, and the master resident, he acts as his own manager; but when the station is large, or the master non-resident, one manager or more is required. The manager acts in all things for the master, and his authority is absolute. It is a responsible situation, requires great experience and tact, and generally commands a good salary. The salary, in many instances, is paid partly in money and partly in stock, which he is permitted to graze on the run; and he is allowed to keep, or he has the use of, several horses. In this way the manager may become in a short time the possessor of a run of his own.

Under the manager there are shepherds, whose duty it is to go out with the sheep in the morning, tend them all day, and return with them to some place of safety at sun-down. One man may shepherd 1,000 sheep; and a man and a boy may safely take the charge of a flock of between 2,000 and 3,000 on a good and well-ordered station. On many stations there are from 10,000 to 40,000 sheep. Hut-men are engaged to keep the huts, and cook, &c., for the shepherds and watchmen. It is, of course, an inferior occupation, and is often performed by old people, partial invalids, and the wives of the shepherds. Married women, whose husbands are employed on the station, are frequently engaged to perform the duties of cook, housemaid, and so on, to the master or manager. The young people, as soon as they can do anything, are set to work; and hence a man with a wife and grown up boys will very readily find employment for himself and all of them on a station. A shepherd receives about £45 per annum and his rations; a shepherd and his wife receive from £55 to £60 per annum and rations; and I have known a shepherd, with wife and two or three boys, receive £100, and all rations supplied.

Stockmen do for cattle what shepherds do for sheep, and they are rarely out of the saddle from morning till night. It is a strange life, and has many attractions for the young and the frivolous. There is not a little art required in tracking the cattle to their feeding grounds, and no small amount of courage is needed to fetch a mob from the mountains, or to entice them from the dense, impenetrable scrub to the muster-grounds, that they may be draughted to market, or have the young among them "branded." I have often admired the young stockman, as he started fresh for his work. He is tall, spare, and bronzed by constant exposure to the sun; *sans* coat and waistcoat, with a leathern belt around his waist, stuck full of "indispensables," bewiskered and moustached; in his hand the stock-whip, and on his head a light straw hat, from beneath which streams his coal-black hair. You have before you the idea of a man who feels himself free, and who has exquisite enjoyment in his freedom. The stockman is generally well mounted, and it is well for him that he is so; for ere he return to the station, he shall have many windings and doublings, gullies to cross, and ridges to ascend and descend, in following and guiding the cattle. It is surprising the distances that cattle will sometimes go, and the inaccessible places they will sometimes choose as their feeding ground. They select their own camping grounds, which are generally on elevated parts, and thither they hie as sunset approaches. The stockman rarely loses himself in the bush, although his way may be trackless; and if he should, the instinct of his horse will bring him home. The pay of the stockman is about £40, with rations, and horse kept up for his use.

In the lambing season all hands on the station are busy, and great is the anxiety of faithful shepherds. Should the weather be broken and wet, or should the feed be less advanced than it should be, many of the lambs die; but this does not often happen. The seasons in Queensland are, upon the whole, favourable to the increase of stock; hence the ratio at which that increase proceeds. But there is another danger that besets the flock at this time; the dingo, or native dog, which is still numerous in the interior, preys on the lambs whenever he finds an opportunity. The dingo has more the appearance of a fox than a dog, and, like his sly compeer, seems to exercise his wits to reach his prey. The shepherds destroy them by shooting, and sometimes by dropping meat impregnated with strychnine near their haunts. A dingo hunt is a very exciting scene, and not unattended by danger; but they are only witnessed now far in the interior.

An additional number of men are required in the season when the washing of the sheep takes place, and much depends on the way in which this work is performed. The good or bad washing gives character, in part, to the clip of wool. Of course, inferior wool will not be changed in its character by the washing, but good wool may be greatly damaged by bad washing.

The shearing of the sheep follows; and this work is performed, not by the shepherds, but by men who devote themselves to that special occupation for a portion of the year. The other parts of the year they act as woodmen, fencers, and shingle splitters. When the season arrives, the "shearers" set off on horseback, carrying with them their few implements and their blanket, for a night cover when they "camp out." They go from station to station, and generally to the same stations year after year. They do their work by the piece, and make a capital thing of it. They have from 4s. 6d. to 5s. per score; and a good workman will pass through his hands from four to five score a day. The wages of other men required about stations are in proportion to those mentioned; and this is the case at the present time, when so many men in Britain are striving to rear a family on 11s. or 13s. a week.

On a well ordered and well-kept station, the clip, that is, the wool of the season, is understood to pay more than the current expenses. There is no rent to pay for dwelling-house, or for as much ground as you like to cultivate for the station use; and the rent of the run is little more, on an average of 14 years, than 12s. per square mile. The squatter has not many calls upon his benevolence, and he can afford to be hospitable. His profits are the increase of the flocks, which, together with the growing surplus arising from the sale of his wool, amounts to good 50 per cent. on his capital.

Besides sheep and cattle, and horses, the climate and pasture of Queensland are well adapted to the support of the llama and alpaca, creatures considerably larger than sheep, and producing a kind of wool much in demand. They have been recently introduced by Mr. Ledger, from South America, after incredible difficulties had been surmounted. The llama is not unlike a small camel, and is used by the inhabitants of Bolivia and Peru as a beast of burden. In Australia it will be better taken care of, and we doubt not will ere long become a source of wealth to its possessors. We shall give an extract from an article that appeared in the *Sydney Morning Herald*, after the flock had been some time depasturing in New South Wales. The date of the paper is August, 1860:—

"The example of sheep farming will naturally prepare us to look favourably on productions of a similar nature—the alpaca wool. We do not think that the discouragements and difficulties which have been incurred by those concerned in its introduction are at all greater than attended the first propagation of our flocks, nor are the two kinds of stock altogether rivals. We see no reason why, with the great variety of herbage produced by this country, and its adaptation to the growth of the alpaca, it should not have a large amount of produce of this kind without decreasing the proportionate quantity of sheep's wool. It seems to be one recommendation that the animals which we have so long desired to introduce, and which are now browsing in the interior, have habits different from those of the sheep, and that they may occupy vacant regions. The following is a calculation made of the probable growth of our alpaca flocks in fifty years—a long time in the life of a man, a short period in the history of a people:—

*Table showing the probable increase of the alpaca flock. The commencement is made with 200 females and 50 males.*

| Females. | Lambs. | Females. | Males. | | | | | | | Males. | Females. | December. |
|---|---|---|---|---|---|---|---|---|---|---|---|---|
| 200 | 120 | 60 | 60 | at 60 p' cent. (allowing 10 per cent. for deaths).. | | | | | | 110 | 280 | 1861 |
| 200 | 120 | 60 | 60 | ,, | ,, | Those drept last year will not lamb | | | | 170 | 320 | 1862 |
| 280 | 160 | 80 | 80 | ,, | ,, | The female lambs 1861 will drop this | | | | 250 | 400 | 1863 |
| 310 | 200 | 100 | 100 | ,, | ,, | ,, | ,, | 1862 | ,, ,, | 350 | 500 | 1864 |
| 420 | 250 | 125 | 125 | ,, | ,, | ,, | ,, | 1863 | ,, ,, | 475 | 625 | 1865 |
| 520 | 260 | 130 | 130 | at 50 p' cent. only | | ,, | ,, | 1864 | ,, ,, | 605 | 775 | 1866 |
| 645 | 320 | 160 | 160 | ,, | ,, | ,, | ,, | 1865 | ,, ,, | 765 | 935 | 1867 |
| 775 | 387 | 190 | 190 | ,, | ,, | ,, | ,, | 1866 | ,, ,, | 955 | 1165 | 1868 |
| 935 | 467 | 235 | 235 | ,, | ,, | ,, | ,, | 1867 | ,, ,, | 1195 | 1400 | 1869 |
| 1322 | 661 | 330 | 330 | ,, | ,, | ,, | ,, | 1868 | ,, ,, | 1520 | 1730 | 1870 |

"There will be, after deduction made for wear and tear, accidents, &c., 3,250, as per above calculation. We further deduct 25 per cent. of total every period of ten years, thus leaving in round numbers 2,500; at same rate, in

| 20 years there would be | ............ | 20,000 |
| 30 ,, ,, | ............ | 160,000 |
| 40 ,, ,, | ............ | 1,280,000 |
| 50 ,, ,, | ............ | 9,760,000 |

"At seven lbs. wool each—68,320,000 lbs., at 2s. per lb., £6,832,000!

"From this it will be seen that making deductions of a liberal nature, according to the present ratio of increase, there will be in fifty years 9,760,000 head, the wool of which, at 2s. per lb., will amount to the sum of £6,832,000 per annum.

"When figures like these are given, incredulity is naturally awakened; but we do not know that there is anything unreasonable in the calculation. At all events, any reasonable reduction may be made, and still leave a value sufficient to deserve the energy and solicitude of the public."

The squatting interest may be said to be entirely in the hands of the British, the few Germans who have small stations being scarcely worth mentioning in this statement; and the principal work on the stations must always be performed by Europeans. Never were the squatters in a more thriving condition, in no colony are there more just squatting laws, and they need neither Chinese nor coolie labour to enable them to develop the wool-producing capabilities of Queensland. When the annual fleece meets the expenses of a sheep station, and the price of sheep is from 10s. to 12s., and the minimum increase in the flocks is 50 per cent., the owners of stations can afford to employ white labour.

## X.—UPS AND DOWNS IN SQUATTING LIFE.

In the previous chapters my aim has been to give some idea of the nature, extent, and reasonable capabilities of the squatting interest in Queensland. The reader must not imagine, however, that squatting life has not its various phases, and the squatting enterprise its own vicissitudes. There was a time when the squatter suffered most severely in all the Australian colonies, and few were able to resist the flood of commercial ruin that swept over the land. Sheep came down to 1s. 6d. a head, and stations went a-begging for occupiers. This disaster was especially felt by the pastoral community in Victoria and New South Wales.

Matters have righted themselves in these colonies, and it is most improbable that such a state of depression and misery will again be experienced. In regard to the colonies named, it may be said that time and experience have done something to consolidate society, and prevent sudden and extensive changes, such as those that produced these disastrous results a few years ago. And, further, the price of sheep can never now descend to such a low figure, since the boiling-down process has fixed the minimum price at 6s. 6d. a head. For a long time it is improbable that the price will become so low; but if it should, it will be arrested there, as it is now ascertained that the tallow and skin of a sheep will fetch in the market on an average 6s. 6d.

In Queensland, stock is not likely to fall much in price for some time, for various reasons. We have seen that there is a vast extent of new country to be taken up, and the stock required will be quite equal to the supply for years to come. Besides, as the population increases,—and it is increasing at a rapid rate—the demand for mutton increases also; but should the price fall to 6s. 6d., then, of course, the boiling-down establishments will be called into requisition again. For some years they have been all but idle, and in several instances have gone to a state of dilapidation, entailing upon their proprietors a heavy loss. But it is better for the colony when the squatter finds a market for his fat sheep in the towns, and for his surplus flocks in the far interior.

I have been over a boiling-down establishment, but the details are too disgusting to put in print. Long may they be superfluous in Queensland; and when they are again called into operation, we shall protect our olfactory nerves against certain powerful odours, and pocket the disgust, because they will save the country from a great disaster. There are some things that give the squatter enterprize in Queensland a great advantage over that of the older colonies. The chief of these are the immense unoccupied country beyond, and the liberal laws under which the squatting leases are granted.

But, notwithstanding, times of trouble may come: large losses may be sustained, sheep and cattle farmers may find their way into the bankruptcy court, and the present 50 per cent. may be converted into an overwhelming deficit. Speculation on a limited capital may do this. Diseases, finding their way among the flocks, may bring this about; a decided fall in the wool market, at some crisis in the history of the station, may accomplish the work; bad seasons may bring it about; and nothing will more certainly produce it than mismanagement.

For some time the squatter has been very successful, but neither is his path always smooth, nor his lot without a "crook," any more than that of others; and if we embrace in our present remarks all the parties connected with squatting, we may say with perfect safety that there are many ups and downs in squatting life.

Many men now acting as shepherds, hut-keepers, and bullock-drivers, in connexion with stations, occupied very different positions at home. A roving and unsettled disposition, generally accompanied with an over-powering passion for strong drink, has brought them to their present state, and the love of the bottle keeps them in it. In many instances these men make good servants, keep them from drink, and over a period of twelve months, they will earn a sum of from £40 to £45. There are cases innumerable in which such men, and others, too, who have under prosperity got into jovial habits, have left the bush with large sums in their "belts," and at the first wayside inn spent every farthing before they moved from the spot; and should they by any chance reach the town, a better fate did not befall them, and they were compelled, under dire necessity, either to take what work cast up on the spot, or return without a "bob" to the station which they had left a few days before.

The process is this: a poor incapable lands in a bar of a public-house; he calls for brandy, and he places in the hands of the bar-man the cheque which he has on the station where he has been serving. He becomes heated with the fiery stimulant, becomes jolly and jovial, and declares that he will "shout" all comers. The meaning of this slang is, that he will treat at his expense all and sundry known or unknown unto him, friend or foe, who shall enter the bar during the process; and the brandy flows like water, and heads grow giddy, and words become high; "fast and furious grows the din;" and if the whole does not end in a "row," it is generally due to the stupifying power of the well-cooked Australian brandy.

Our poor incapable is tumbled into bed, and the cheque is safe in mine host's strong box.

In the morning the wretched man calls for brandy, and still more brandy, which is freely given him; and for two or three days matters go on thus, till the demand is resisted, and the poor drunkard, now on the verge of *delirium tremens*, is told that his money is exhausted, and that, should he not instantly "take himself off," he shall be kicked out of doors.

The law cannot reach such cases; and so long as men shall be such consummate fools, the low villanous grog-seller will pluck them with impunity.

But there are "ups" as well as "downs" in squatting life, and several of these have come under my observation. Of course, many men engaged in this work have gradually risen from poverty to affluence. Many, who began with very small capitals indeed, have ended by possessing thousands of pounds. This has hitherto been the rule in Queensland, and so far as we can judge, it is probable that it will continue to be the rule.

One day I was met by a gentleman from the bush, who freely entered into conversation. I had at one time made a short voyage with him on board a steamer, and had thus come to know him a little. "I have just sold my station," said he.

"Well," said I, "I hope you have made something good of it."

"Yes, I believe I have," was his reply.

"You squatters are the men to make money in this colony," was my rejoinder.

"I don't know, but I have received £29,000 cash, and a bill for £1,000."

I expressed my surprise.

"I am going to retire," said my friend, "and devote myself to the education of my family."

I heartily approved and commended the resolution.

This gentleman had not himself got a liberal education, and knowing the many and great disadvantages the want of a thorough course of instruction and training entails upon a man, he was determined that his sons should not labour under the same defect. I was told that this gentleman was a journeyman mechanic some 15 years before. He had certainly followed the squatting to some purpose.

I shall give another case, the type of many. My duties required me at one time to pay a visit, of a few days, to one of the richest agricultural districts of New South Wales. I came in contact with many shopkeepers, woodmen, and farmers. They were all well-to-do in the world, and lived like little potentates, each on his own domain. I was specially interested in the farmers, and enjoyed the hearty hospitality of several of them. The history of most of them was told in my hearing; that of one I shall briefly rehearse.

About ten years previous to the date of my visit, this man had left one of the rural districts of Scotland, accompanied by his wife and several young children. Arrived in Australia, he at once hired himself as a shepherd, and his wife took the situation of cook to the master, who happened to live a good portion of the year on the station. The children, who were all girls, managed themselves. In the course of two or three years, what between the wages of both, none of which was spent, but all laid out in sheep as it was due, and the annual increase of his little flock, he soon found himself in possession of between £300 and £400. His great ambition now was to buy a farm, where he could take up his abode, cultivate the soil, and keep two or three cows, and feed poultry and pigs. In this way he fancied he would be able to keep his family in a respectable position.

I spent a day with this worthy man on his farm, and had the whole corroborated by himself. And he told me that his farm consisted of upwards of 300 acres of good land, on which he grew a quantity of wheat and potatoes, but which he chiefly used for grazing a number of cows, whose produce paid him very well. In this case, as in many others, I was pleased to know that in prosperity my friend had not forgotten the gratitude and the honour due to God. A steady and liberal supporter of a Christian congregation two or three miles from his farm, he had at the same time opened his dining-room for a Sunday school, where the children all round were weekly taught the holy doctrines of our blessed religion by the daughters of this erewhile Scottish peasant.

## XI.—A FEW DAYS ON THE PINE RIVER.

It was a beautiful morning that on which a friend and myself, both well mounted, set out for the Pine River. Arrayed in broad Panama hats with wreaths of muslin, we set the rays of the sun at defiance; and to add the more to our bodily comfort, the coat and waistcoat were wrapped in the camping blanket, which was strapped to the saddle. For several miles the track —for no road is yet formed so far from towns—leads across an interminable series of ridges, most of them strewed over with sharp quartzy gravel; and as you reach their northern termination, some exhibit tokens of iron-stone and dark shales.

The ridges are bare and verdureless, covered with the never-failing gum tree, iron-bark, wattle, and box tree; and the narrow winding valleys between are covered with a rich and beautiful vegetation. As we approach the South Pine, the country becomes level, the soil light, the feed pretty good, and one meets with small herds of cattle grazing about very quietly, proof enough that they are not unaccustomed to equestrians. On the immediate banks of the South Pine, which is past by ford, and, except in flood times, contains almost no water, there is some very rich alluvial soil, which is at present covered by a dense scrub.

A few days before we passed, some mischievous blacks from the north had speared a bullock that belonged to a squatter whom they did not like, and devoured the carcass. Afterwards they betook themselves to the impenetrable scrubs that skirt the river, into which neither white nor black police dare follow them. They will not do this to the squatter who treats them kindly, and deals with them truthfully, as we learned a day or two afterwards.

Between the South and North Pine the land lies low, is thickly wooded, much of it is covered with long coarse grass, and is, in many parts, better fitted for the support of the marsupial tribes than that of cattle or horses. On the North Pine the soil assumes a very different character, and the country becomes quite interesting to the traveller. Long green ridges stretch away on every side; the timber is not so dense; the grass is of a much finer and richer quality, and it appears capable of supporting a large number of cattle. Sheep are not kept here, except in such numbers only as supply the domestic necessities of the station. Both cattle and horses were in fine condition, and the station masters were in good heart. Some of the views on the Pine were very beautiful, full of the most delicious repose, and reminded me much of some of the river scenery in the lowlands of Scotland.

The bush, or general forest, is here the same as everywhere else, stamped with the most provoking sameness. You think that every weather-beaten gum, or lofty fluted iron bark, is the fac-simile of every tree of the same species you passed since you started from Brisbane. The srub is very dense and very beautiful in some parts of the course of the river, and the scrub lands are peculiarly rich. Never did I experience the attacks of the mosquitoes so severe and unendurable as in one of the magnificent scrubs in that district. After breakfast I had strolled away to quietly examine the rich and peculiar vegetation. I had found my way into a part where the rays of the sun were completely excluded by the dense, marvellously interwoven vegetation that formed a dark magnificent canopy over head. Around me were hanging in thousands the tendrils of the creeping or rather climbing plants, varying in thickness from that of a telegraphic wire to the cable of a ship, and from forty to sixty feet in length. The whole thing, canopy and tendrils, was supported by the enormous trees that grew at intervals, and whose tops had become matted together, although their great trunks stood far apart. Many of these climbing plants bear a beautiful flower, but the flowering time was over at the period of my visit. I had not been many minutes in this position, till I was fairly beaten off by the voracious attack of the mosquitoes, both black and grey, and was glad to make with all convenient speed for the open bush. What surprised me was, that at this time I slept several nights in succession, in an open wooden house, little over half a mile from this spot, without even the use of mosquito curtains. I have, however, in other parts of the country, experienced something similar. These pests to all new comers do not always make their appearance in the same place, and at the same time; although, doubtless, they even are regulated by laws too subtle for us to recognise always, yet they often appear to act very capriciously; and one, when smarting under their irritating bite, is sometimes led to think with the poor negro when he expressed his wonder what the object might be that the Maker of all had in view when He created mosquitoes. This little busy, troublesome, bloodthirsty creature is, however, worst on new arrivals; in a short time it either does not bite you at all, or you become impervious to any bad consequences arising from it.

In travelling through the bush, one often meets with traces of the English bee; it was introduced at an early period, has multiplied vastly, and has spread over a marvellous extent of country. The English bee thrives very well in the colony, and produces a large quantity of honey. The flavour, I used to think, was scarcely so delicate as that of good home honey; but there is a native bee as well, and it too is very plentiful. It is a very small dark brown creature with glossy wings, and it invariably builds its nest high in the clefts and openings of trees. The aborigines are excessively fond of the honey of the wild bee, which is of a dark colour, very pure, but of a slightly coarse flavour. The way the blacks, and after them the whites, obtain the honey is somewhat ingenious. The bee is so small, that you cannot see it with the naked eye a few feet above you. How, then, is the black fellow to ascertain whether a certain tree contains a hive or not?

On one occasion I was riding through the bush in company with a young man, the son of a farmer, and our conversation ranged over such subjects as the scene and circumstances suggested.

"How does the black fellow know for certain that such and such a tree contains a hive, and not the others?" said I to my companion.

"Very easily," said he; and as we passed along, I observed his sharp eye scanning the upper boughs of the huge trees. In a few moments he reined up his horse, and said, "Come here; take the position I now occupy, and direct your eye steadily towards the large bough on your right, about forty feet upwards, and tell me whether you see any object."

I looked, and, sure enough, I saw at the point indicated what appeared to be a mass of scales dancing in the sun. It was the sun-light playing on the wings of the bees as they swarmed about the opening, eagerly pressing for admittance with their loads of plunder.

"Ah!" said I, "I see it all now. Well, there can be no mistake when the sun shines."

"No; and in this land, as you shall know, sunshine is the rule."

When the blacks meet with a hive in their wanderings in the bush, they either climb the tree by notching it with their tomahawk and cut it out, or they set to and cut the tree down. The labour is nothing to these wild sons of nature, who wield their little weapons with great dexterity; and when the tree is prostrate, they can extract their prize more dexterously and with less waste. Of few things are the aborigines careful, and they know nothing of economy; but on no account would they lose a drop of the honey of the wild bee, and even the bark in which they preserve what they are not able to eat at the time is steeped in water, and the water drunk.

On my visit to the Pine River I was much interested in what I saw of the blacks, and was told by the kind-hearted squatter with whom I stayed regarding them. He assured me that the blacks a little to the north on the coast cherished very hostile feelings towards the whites; but, he added, they discriminate between their friends and their enemies—between those who are faithful and kind to them, and those who break faith with them, and treat them harshly. He was under no apprehension, as the blacks far and near knew him, and had perfect confidence in his sincere good feeling. As a proof of the active existence of both feelings in the untutored breasts of these savages, I may state that two hundred had only a week before camped on this gentleman's run, and several of them visited his house to assure him that none of his cattle should be injured, "because he was black fellow's friend;" but they vowed vengeance on those who "hated black fellow, and shot him dead."

Many have been the quarrels that have taken place on stations between the whites and the blacks, and often these have ended tragically. It is perhaps impossible to know the actual beginnings, but there is no doubt on the minds of most men that the whites are generally the aggressors. These occurrences are not so frequent as they used to be, and when they do take place, a more searching investigation is made than was wont to be in the olden time. My own experience of the aborigines of Queensland is, that they are indolent, inoffensive, good-humoured, and not destitute of a certain rude politeness. They are great cowards for a gun or a dog, but will think nothing of appropriating such an article as an axe, without any compunction. There is little independence of spirit among them, yet I have heard of one black fellow who accosted a white man cutting down a tree in the bush thus:—"What for white fellow cut down tree? tree no white fellow's; tree black fellow's." And raising himself to his utmost height, and spreading his arms wide, and rolling his large black eyes about with a wild fire, he added—"All fellow trees black fellow's." The poor savage meant by this grand natural gesture and these meagre words, that the white man was an intruder, and that the tree to which he had laid the axe and all the trees of the bush, yea, the country itself, belonged to the black man. The savage is right, but might is on the side of the intruder.

A station

verted into butter or cheese, presents a very stirring scene in the morning. On the occasion of my visit, I was up betimes to see all that was to be seen, even though, at that time, the thought of writing a book had never darkened my mental vision, or disturbed my midnight slumbers. A bit of advice to all who may emigrate :—Be observant; keep your eyes wide open; acquaint yourself with everything; but do not thereby prevent yourself from the timely and energetic discharge of duty.

At six, or somewhat earlier, the milking commences. The master, in many instances, does this work himself,—women seldom do it in the colony; a lad, or black fellow, conveys the milk in pails to the dairy, where the mistress receives it in charge. The processes of butter-making and cheese-making go on in the early morning in the coolest place in the station, two or three times in the week, and, in many instances, every lawful morning. About the half of the milk that each cow yields is left for the good of the calf, which very speedily helps itself to its share, as the cow, when dismissed from the "bail," the place where she is fixed to be milked, is turned into the stock-yard, where the hungry calves have been all night. It is quite a sight to see two or three dozen sleek and lively creatures at their morning meal. The calves grow up and increase the herd by at least 50 per cent. per annum; and the cheese and the butter are transferred at short intervals, often on horses' backs, to the nearest town. The cheese is poor, and draws about 9d. per pound; the butter is good, and generally fetches from 2s. to 2s. 6d. per pound.

On such a station as this, pigs and poultry are abundant, are well fed, and meet with a ready market at prices of which you hear no complaints. When in the neighbourhood of a salt-water creek, where the fish is abundant, the industrious farmer sometimes adds to his other avocations that of fish-curer. The fish is very good, and, prepared thus, meets with a ready and remunerative sale in the towns.

Anxious to see the character of the run, I willingly accepted the invitation of my kind host to accompany him on his tour of inspection. We were five hours in the saddle, and during that time you may suppose that we went over a considerable space. The portion of the run we traversed was, in many parts of it, exceedingly like an English park on a magnificent scale. The timber was by no means so heavy as it is near Brisbane, and in many parts there were not many large trees to the acre. The surface was diversified somewhat, but was all covered with an abundant feed. Here and there were undulating ridges of light soil, and near to the mouth of the river there was some swampy land; but the vast proportion of the run over which I rode was composed of some of the finest soil I had met with in Queensland. It is not black mould, but a soil of a deep red colour, and can scarcely be excelled for agricultural purposes. In other parts of the colony I have seen the finest crops growing on the same kind of soil. On the Pine River, and in all other parts of the colony where I have seen it, I observed that it lay in extended plateaux, through which the streams, when flooded, had cut many deep trenches, or miniature ravines. You cannot imagine anything in the agricultural way more enticing to the farmer than these vast plateaux; and as I rode along, my fancy pictured them covered with the Sea Island cotton-plant, and a busy and happy population picking and securing the precious fibre. The fancy is about to become reality, for I observe, since my return, that this very district, and lands further to the north, have been proclaimed an agricultural reserve. If all the other reserves are chosen with equal judgment, as I have no doubt they are, the home population who avail themselves of the "free grants" have a good prospect before them.

The kangaroo, opossum, flying-fox, kangaroo-rat, and other minor game, abound in these unmolested parts; and the various common birds, too, seemed to be fairly represented. We came in contact with an "old-man kangaroo," as the large males are designated by the bushmen, with whom I was not a little amused. We were walking our horses, and came upon him feeding quietly in company with what appeared to us to be some four or five females, whom he obviously considered under his protection. He allowed us to approach within a few yards, and then jumped, or, as we would say in Scotland, "bobbed," on in the rear of his party. This he did several times; and at last, dreading some danger, although, poor brute, he was safe enough in our neighbourhood, and had nothing in the world to dread from us, he increased the speed, and lengthened the span of his leaps, till he bounded like what I had never before witnessed, over the ridge, and down by the densely-wooded banks of the river.

Often he sat erect to look and to listen; and on such occasions he pricked his full ears, and his short fore-feet hung pendant, the very embodiment of physical *fecklessness*. The kangaroo, in jumping, does not use its fore limbs, but holds them close to the chest, with the paws hanging down. Nor does it use its enormous tail, as many suppose. The tail is used simply as a balance, and never touches the ground except when feeding, or when sitting erect. The whole weight of the body in jumping is received on the very powerful lower joints of the hind legs. I can now fancy the excitement and zest of a kangaroo hunt, although I have never witnessed one.

My companion was naturally led to tell me some of the exploits of these "old men of the wood," when closely pressed by the dogs, kept and trained for the special hunt, in which he had often taken part. Young and inexperienced dogs not unfrequently meet with their death, or are maimed for life, by these powerful creatures, when hard pressed. If they come within reach, they are almost certain to be ripped up by one jerk of the principal claw on the hind foot, which they use as the chief weapon of defence, and a powerful one it is. Old dogs will rarely attack the kangaroo when at bay; they rather dog his steps, and weary him out by a series of annoying side attacks. Old kangaroos have been known to wile the dogs to water-holes, where they often succeed in effecting their escape. Indeed, they always take to the water when within reach; and many a good kangaroo hound has lost its life by following them. The knowing old fellows plunge into the water, and, with fore paws expanded, await their pursuers. Should the temper of the dog urge him to follow, the "old man" receives him in his powerful embrace, and presses him under water till he is suffocated.

During the time of my visit, there was a small native camp in the immediate neighbourhood of the house. I could see their fires and hear their constant chatter through the chinks of my bed-room door. The blacks were perfectly inoffensive, except in their nasty habits, and several of them did little light jobs on the station. I interested myself in watching their movements, and noting their habits and occupations. Early in the morning, the men who were not engaged doing anything for the squatter went out to fish and hunt, and returned at sun-down, bearing with them the game they had caught. The fish they take with nets, made by the gins or married women, of grass, on the same principle as those that are used by fishermen on our own shores, or by placing innumerable twigs across some shallow part of the creek at high water, and when the tide returns, the water passes through, but the fish are detained. They obtain the game by tracking them to their places of shelter, generally in the excavations of large trees, and then cutting them out with their small hand axe or tomahawk, without which no black ever travels.

I was present on one occasion when the party returned, and shall tell you exactly what took place. The sun had gone down, and black night was creeping over the bush. The trunks of the great weather-beaten trees appeared grotesque and fearsome in the flickering glare of the camp fires. The gins and the picciniunies (black children) were squatting around, and retain their positions. The men cast upon the ground the fish and the other items of which they were possessed. Then followed a species of consultation, which was wholly incomprehensible to me, but was understood by my friend, who was well acquainted with their language. The upshot was, that the best of the fish was offered in barter for damper, and beef, and tea. The bargain was struck, the blacks received a good supper, and we a delicious accompaniment to damper and tea next morning. The remainder of the fish was cast upon the fire, roasted, and devoured without further ado, or any preparation. The only thing they had caught in the shape of game was a kangaroo-rat, a creature about the size of a rabbit; and I shall never forget the look of contempt which one of the sable ladies gave as she seized the rat, examined its qualities, and then threw it, with the utmost *nonchalance*, on the glowing embers. For a moment she allowed it to be enveloped in the ruddy glow, then turned it (still contemptuously) with a stick, then seized it and scraped it all over with her long skinny fingers. On the fire it was cast again, and allowed to broil for a minute or two, then it was removed to undergo the process of opening. The viscera was taken out, and the cavity was filled with grass. The carcass was again placed on the fire, remained a few moments, was then removed, torn in pieces, and devoured. The entire operation was performed by the skinny fingers of the gin, and the process did not take much more time than I take to rehearse it. Thus passed off the only aboriginal supper of which I was witness, although one often encounters the blacks at their stray meals.

The after talk was not a little amusing, and not altogether void of interest. Inferior though the aboriginal be to the white man, who is gradually appropriating his country, yet he is "a man and a brother;" and, however degraded, you cannot but experience some interest when you see indications of awakening intelligence and rationality. We talked about various things, chiefly about where they had been, what they had seen, and what they could do. Only one young man had the least glimmering of anything spiritual or religious, or showed the least desire to know anything higher than themselves. This person, I was told, would sometimes put a question regarding the Maker of white men, and the rivers, and the kangaroos, and the thunder; and he had come to understand that drinking, and swearing, and stealing were offensive to the Good One. My opinion is, from all that I have seen, that minds of a sanguine nature, who have spoken or written on the subject of the aborigines of North Australia, have attributed to them more notions of spiritual things than they really possess. It is very sad, but is notwithstanding a fact, account for it as we may, and abuse it though some do.

My friend, willing to give me as much insight of their characters, and habits, and notions as possible, drew them out into conversation. One fellow, with a cowardly look, although he was a great boaster, and whom I had seen making spears and waddies the day before, desired him to tell white fellow (myself) that those weapons I had seen him making were intended to kill certain men of another tribe; and he poised the weapon the while, with the utmost grace, to show me how he should effect his purpose. This was all "bounce" before "white fellow." The same genius laid claim to be a "rain maker," and he managed to keep up the deception among a few; but his explanation of his superior and supernatural claims was so confused and absurd, that I could make neither head nor tail of it.

When we were about to retire, three of the young men quite took me by surprise by striking up "Auld Langsyne!" They sung it well; and when a homely Scotch word dropt from their memories, they put in one of their own, thus preserving the tune, whatever havoc might be made of the sense. At this time, I had not been long in the colony, and, separated as I was from every relative I had on earth, this slight incident started a train of thought, and opened a fountain of feeling, neither of which did I wish disturbed that night.

## XII.—THE DESIDERATUM.

Squatting is certainly at present the staple of Queensland, and for a long while it will retain the ascendancy. We can anticipate a time, however, and believe in its realization, if this new colony shall be conducted for a series of years with an equal amount of political wisdom as that which has characterized its commencement, when the agricultural interest will be second only (if second) to the pastoral. The two systems are not, as many persons, especially among the ill-informed on both sides, seem to think, of antagonistic nature. They are, in truth, but the parts of one great system, whereby the large resources of the colony are to be developed. The one is the complement of the other. Neither, without the other, is perfect. The world's history shows us that the one follows hard on the heels of the other, and in numerous instances has overtaken and surpassed its predecessor. We have the pastoral; why should we not make an effort to produce the agricultural? It will come. The sooner it comes, the better for the colony, and in some important respects, as we shall see, the better for Old England herself. In fact, we consider the introduction of an agricultural population the desideratum of the day as it regards Queensland.

Say that the colony, in its length and its breadth, were in the hands of the squatters, and that every acre had its estimated complement of stock, would any man presume to affirm that that colony was yielding up to man the abundant resources with which it has been endowed by a beneficent Providence? There would be abundance of wool, very much tallow, hides, and hoofs, and horns without number, and mountains of bones would flank the boiling-down establishments; but after all, what is this, as a final result, in comparison with the treasures which the hand of honest industry might gather under the combined influence of a rich soil and a genial clime?

Every person who desires the prosperity of Queensland, must wish success to its agriculture. On the one side of our banner there is the stimulating motto—ADVANCE AUSTRALIA; on the other let us inscribe in letters of gold one more homely and not less significant—SPEED THE PLOUGH. There is room enough for both squatter and farmer; and whilst the one sends home to the English market the cleanest and the finest wool he can produce, let the other be encouraged to supply the looms of Manchester and Glasgow with the fine cotton fibre which our extensive sea-board is capable of growing.

In order to accomplish this, many thousands of industrious families must be induced to settle in those districts where agricultural operations of a nature suited to the soil and climate are most likely to prosper; and there are many such districts in Queensland. The entire surplus population of the kind referred to, that England could supply for years to come, might be disposed of there with incalculable advantage to the colony, and very palpable advantage to themselves. A numerous class of small proprietors resident on and cultivating their own farms would be the making of this new country. When a man has an interest in the soil as a proprietor, it effects a salutary change in all his views, and he becomes an excellent citizen and a devoted patriot. This is the material of which the substratum of society should be composed; and as is the character of the foundation, so will be the structure raised upon it. You may fill the country with Chinamen and coolies, but these will never constitute a colony worthy of the name of British; and this magnificent country would in that case be handed over to a few great capitalists, who would grow cotton as the squatters produce wool, and, both being generally absentees, the population would consist mainly of sheep and Asiatics.

We have no special objection to the introduction of Chinese and coolies by the employers of labour on their own account;

but we deprecate the employment of labour falling into the hands of a few moneyed men, who have no possible interest in the country, except it be to extract the greatest possible amount of money at the least possible outlay, for the purpose of keeping up expensive establishments in other countries. There is a tendency in the squatting system in this direction; but under wise political laws and enlightened social and commercial arrangements, this tendency will be checked, and the squatter will become a resident on the soil more generally than he is at present. Entrust the production of cotton to great capitalists, entirely by coolie or Chinese labour, and you vastly increase the evil of absenteeism, and fix it as a curse and a permanent blight on one of the finest colonies under the British crown.

The employment of labour in such a colony as Queensland should be in as many hands as possible; in this way alone will you succeed in securing a resident proprietary, and the expenditure of the money of the colony for the development still farther of its resources. The proprietary of which I speak may either work with their own hands, or they may employ what labour, black or white, they like, according to their ability; or they may do both, which appears to us the most feasible of all plans that have been broached. But you can only secure such a proprietary by inducing the industrious families who have difficulty in living at home to emigrate to the colony.

This is, indeed, the desideratum,—a large industrious proprietary, each resident on his own freehold farm, using his own head and hands, the hands of his grown family, and as many more, black or white, as it suited him, to develop the resources of the soil. These would constitute the yeomen of Queensland, the very heart and soul of the country. This is the class that Victoria and New South Wales are so desirous to have established on their rich valleys and wheat-producing plains. This is the class that has given stability and reasonable prosperity to South Australia, after the disasters that followed quick on the blunders by which the commencement of that colony was characterized. This is the class that has converted Tasmania into a great agricultural country. This is the class, too, that has raised New Zealand to the position which it now occupies as a grain-producing colony. And what would any of these colonies speedily become, were this class of industrious small proprietors, who think it no degradation to work with their own hands, to be withdrawn, and their places supplied by a few great squatters or cotton cultivators? What would England herself be without her stout-hearted yeomen?

By every legitimate means, therefore, this class of emigrants should be induced to go to Queensland. None would derive more benefit from the change than they themselves and their families; and in no other way, keeping before our minds past colonial experience, and the common sense view of things, can the resources of such a colony as Queensland be perfectly developed. Besides producing wool, and cotton, and sugar, all of which could be done by the non-resident capitalist, there are many other articles which the country is capable of producing, and which could be cultivated only by such a resident population as we desiderate. And, in addition to this, is it not a consideration of vast importance to Britain, that here, in Queensland, one of the healthiest colonies in the world, and one of the richest, any number of her hard-worked and under-paid population may find a comfortable home? And whilst they supply the raw materials for her looms, they create a new outlet for many of her manufactures. A colony of Chinamen and coolies will be poor customers to the manufacturers of Manchester, Glasgow, and Leeds, in comparison with a population of British origin and with British tastes.

That there is abundance of agricultural land in Queensland on which to place such a population as this, is well known, although for a long time this was denied, and even yet you may meet with some well-to-do squatter, or speculator in stock, who affirms the contrary. The Report of the Committee of Assembly, published in 1860, and the experience of many small farmers in the neighbourhood of all the towns, prove this beyond all doubt. And Government have adopted the most effectual method of settling this question, by having had large districts of country in several parts of the colony surveyed, with the view of industrious families settling thereon, for the special purpose of cultivating the soil. At the time we write, there are eleven such reserves surveyed, and open to purchasers, together containing nearly 200,000 acres of first-rate agricultural land.

There is room, then, for any number of industrious families who shall give their energies to agricultural pursuits in Queensland; and every facility is afforded them by Government, the nature and the value of which will be better understood by the home reader when he has perused the chapters that follow. In these chapters, too, he will have placed before him, in as much detail as my space will admit of, both the kind of work he will have to do, and the probable remuneration the various products of the soil are likely to yield. My work done,—which is to place before the public the claims of a new and little known British colony,—I shall feel satisfied that I have done my duty, both to the colony and my fellow countrymen, and shall leave every man to judge for himself.

## XIII.—WHAT WILL THE COLONY GROW?

This question will naturally occur to those who have some thoughts about emigrating; and a very reasonable question it is. To one who has been in the colony, and observed what is going on there, and the nature and variety of the products gathered by the energetic and planning farmer, the question that is suggested is rather this—"What will the colony *not* grow?" There is a combination of circumstances in favour of Queensland, as a field for agricultural pursuits, by small freehold farmers, which exists in few other countries.

First of all, the climate, though warm, is very healthy, and Europeans, with ordinary care, can work in the field all the year over, when their labour is required, with impunity. I am aware that parties are at the present time making strong statements to the contrary; but this does not affect my remarks, for they are made on the ground of competent testimony, observation, and experience, all of which have been more fully detailed under the head of climate. Then, the soil is varied, much of it light, but much also very rich, and largely productive. It ranges from light quick loams, through all the varieties of friable clays, to the richest vegetable mould. Very much of the land, especially in the interior, is fit only for grazing purposes; but it will be a long while before the proper agricultural lands are exhausted. The geographical position of the country, being partly within and partly without the tropics, contributes largely to the productiveness of the soil. The rainy seasons, on the one hand, are more broken up and distributed than in thorough tropical regions; and the long droughts and hot winds of the southern colonies, on the other, are all but unknown. The consequence is, that the country is always green, and the crops are not arrested. Failures will, of course, sometimes take place in crops quite suited to the soil and climate, but that is rare when justice is done by the husbandman; and, as a matter of course, failures often take place when crops unsuited to the soil and climate are persisted in.

The bush lands, that is, the open forest lands, along the coast for hundreds of miles, and inland for about 50, are well adapted to the cultivation of the cotton plant, the sugar-cane, the coffee, and tobacco shrubs, and all sorts of textile plants, from which paper and cordage may be produced in any quantities. The undulating country, covered in many places with a soil, the *débris* of old slates and shales, will grow the grape and the pine-apple to perfection. The scrub lands, that is, those numerous low, level patches by the margins of rivers and creeks, above high-water mark, clothed with the most luxuriant and beautiful vegetation, composed of black unctuous clay and vegetable mould, will grow anything that may be cast into them by the hand of man—all the better should a system of draining be adopted. The extensive plateaux in many parts of the sea-board, obviously old sea-marks, of a deep chocolate colour, but little understood as yet, will produce magnificent crops of Sea Island cotton, and all kinds of fruit; while in the interior, within the moist influence of the mountain ranges, where the temperature is moderate, wheat is grown equal at least to that which is produced in South Australia, New Zealand, or Van Dieman's Land.

The capabilities are great, and the range of product is also great. On the same farm you may see growing, side by side, maize, peas, potatoes, oats, coffee, sugar-cane, arrowroot, ginger, flax, cotton, peaches, oranges, apricots, figs, mulberries, grapevines, pine-apples, and bananas. All these may be seen growing to perfection in the open air, and under any ordinary treatment, in the neighbourhood of Brisbane. And should the reader still put the question, "What does the colony grow?" I might add several items to the above list.

The agriculture of Queensland is in its very infancy, and partakes of the imperfections and defects of an infantile state. But under proper treatment it will speedily get over these, and rise to the importance to which it is destined to attain. Queensland will one day take a high place, in regard to agriculture as well as to pastoral avocations, among the Australian colonies. But before this is realized, we must have an influx of the right sort of emigrants, and those who are at present engaged on the soil will require to manifest more energy and enterprise. Those who have begun to cultivate the soil have, in many instances, much to unlearn; and all new comers have much to learn, even though they may have been connected with the agricultural interests at home. In point of fact, agriculture on scientific principles is yet to begin in Queensland, for the present tiller of the soil, if he may have come from Essex or from Lothian, follows in the footsteps of his father or grandfather, regardless alike of the difference of soil, and cereal, and climate; and many a time he has had no closer relation to the soil in his native land than that sustained by the country tailor or cobbler.

On one occasion, when talking with a person who had been some years in the colony, our conversation turned on agriculture.

"Ah, sir," said he, "agriculture will never do here. There is no use in trying."

"What!" said I, "do you mean to say that that beautiful soil I pass over, by the banks of these creeks, every day I ride a few miles into the bush, is of no value for agricultural purposes, and is destined only to feed the kangaroo, or support the townspeoples' cows and calves."

"I mean to say, sir," he replied, with great pomposity and wounded vanity,—"I mean to say, sir, that farming in this colony will not do; in proof of which, sir, I myself have tried it, and failed."

This seemed perfectly satisfactory to his mind, and possibly might have some influence with others, who were not competent to form a judgment for themselves; but with me it went for nothing. Nor will it have much weight with any of my readers, when I tell them that my friend was a craftsman of limited celebrity, and in any town in Scotland would have been called a "daidlin body;" in plain English, a handless, good-for-nothing creature. On statements such as these, by writers equally incompetent, made to friends at home, and in the other colonies, through their correspondence, is the character of a new country misrepresented, traduced, and damaged. First impressions are abiding, and the first impressions of Queensland, as a country fitted to bring to profitable perfection its own peculiar products, should be favourable.

We want men for this colony who know the difference between vegetable mould and clay when they see them—who understand that climate must regulate crop—who will watch the seasons and forecast the probable demand for their produce—who will follow neither their incapable neighbour, nor their antiquated grandfather, but who have sufficient moral courage to act on their own matured judgment, founded on experience and observation in connexion both with soil and climate. I should sincerely rejoice to see the weaver, the tailor, the shoemaker bettering his circumstances by betaking himself to the soil; but if he neglect the reasonable conditions, or if he be incompetent, he must not expect to realize a fortune as a farmer, nor must he represent far and near that *his* failure forsooth is a proof that the boundless lands of the colony are good for nothing but to feed cattle or sheep.

The colony can produce many things; and the men who win their bread by the sweat of their brow, who have a head to plan and hands to work, can alone provide the kind of labour, to whose steady application it will give forth the treasures it contains. It matters not to which of the handicrafts they may belong; it matters not whether they may have followed the plough, cast the drain, stood at the bench, worked at the forge, sat on the board, plied the shuttle, or dug in the mine; if furnished with the indispensable moral qualities, and physical powers, they are the men who shall take their place with success in the agricultural enterprise of Queensland.

## XIV.—COTTON SUPPLY.

For several years, considerable anxiety has been felt regarding the supply of cotton, and some attempts have been made to increase the number of sources whence it might be drawn. Far-seeing men, when they contemplated the daily development of the trade in cotton stuffs, and thought of England being dependent on sources foreign to herself for the supply of the raw material, naturally entertained a certain amount of anxiety. Perhaps it scarcely took shape in most minds; it existed as a vague uneasiness; it required something of a decisive nature to give it form, to convert it into a motive to action.

Recent events, and events still pending, the effects of which in a commercial point of view, no man can forsee, furnish a motive of sufficient strength to urge the cotton lords of Lancashire, and all parties interested in the prosperity of our great manufacturing enterprise, to take action in this matter. The civil war in America, whatever be its consequences to the American people, has certainly taught us the folly and the danger of depending on strangers for an article of such vital importance as cotton. But whether it shall rouse John Bull thoroughly to action, is another and very different question.

Up to a very recent date, America supplied us with eight-tenths of the fibre used in the cotton manufactures of Britain; and although the relative proportions from this and from other countries are daily changing, yet such a state of matters gives that country much more power over our great national interests than should be allowed, except under the direst necessity.

There are few questions of more vital importance to the mother country than that of the supply of cotton. Much of her wealth, and not a little of her influence among the nations of the world, depend upon it. With it, therefore, is closely bound up our national progress and prosperity. But the supply hitherto has been almost exclusively from countries over which we have no control, and must therefore be, at the best, subject to too many contingencies. Is it wise in Britain to remain dependent on the foreigner for the supply of such an article? The growing impression on the public mind undoubtedly is, that it is not. And from many indications—from the meetings that are being held in the manufacturing districts—from an extensive correspondence in the newspapers—from the able articles that are appearing in the most influential organs of public opinion—from the associations that are coming into existence—it is very obvious that this subject is not merely agitating the surface, but moving to its depths the mind of a large portion of the English public. But whether this shall lead to decided action, and whether that action shall be in the right direction, is yet to be proved. Much talk about it is good to create, and spread, and sustain an interest; but mere talk is useless. Subscribing money to purchase cotton from the native producers, and to assist experiments in new fields, may be very laudable, and may effect a fractional amount of good; but we respectfully submit that this goes a short way to meet the case, and to secure a result worthy of the interests at stake. Even the proposal, which meets with so much favour in England, to import Chinese and coolies to those countries connected with the British crown, where cotton may be grown does not, in our judgment, come up to the exigencies of the case.

In the English mind, the question is too much one of pounds, shillings, and pence. Now, although it must, of necessity, be viewed very much in this light, yet why narrow the ground to this one issue? In our peculiar circumstances, as possessed of an extensive colonial empire, as having a yearly surplus of population to dispose of, why not associate the demand for cotton supply with the necessity for emigration? Is it not worth our while to inquire whether the wise direction of the one might not, in great measure, furnish us with what we want of the other? If our own surplus industrious population could be got to produce, in part at least, the cotton fibre we must have for our numerous looms, we should then secure a three-fold result, the consequences of which no man could over-estimate: There would be a great reduction of contingencies, the maximum stability in the supply would be gained; the surplus and underpaid labour would be well provided for, and the labour market at home would never be glutted; the manufacturers would find in such a population a valuable and constantly augmenting market for their various fabrics. We should like to see the question discussed on this broad ground.

Meanwhile, if we mistake not, the only question that weighs

with the public is, where shall we get our cotton for the smallest possible sum per pound? This, we admit, is the first and the most important question; but it is by no means the only one of importance that demands our consideration at such a crisis. We want upwards of one thousand millions of pounds weight of cotton per annum to keep our looms going, and we want it at the lowest possible figure; but we also want the supply to be subject to as few fluctuations and contingencies as possible. Of this quantity, America, in 1859, furnished upwards of eight hundred millions; the remainder was derived from India, West Indies, Brazil, the Mediterranean, and one or two other countries.

It is not wise to depend so entirely on any one country, not under British control, for such a large proportion of this indispensable staple. Whither, then, shall we turn our eyes? What country or countries may be expected to respond to our call?

Some look to Africa, and they imagine that a large supply may be procured from the tribes on the Zambesi and its tributaries, and from the free blacks, whom British philanthropy, with its usual largeness of heart, proposes to reinstate in their own country. These schemes may or may not come up to expectation, but even though a large supply could be produced in this field, where is our guarantee that it would be steady? You may enter into arrangements; you may make certain stipulations; but should these wayward tribes become jealous, mischievous, or refractory, who is to enforce the conditions? However fair may be the prospect in this direction, however certain it may be that much cotton may be produced, yet you can't command a regular supply, because you have no real power over the producers.

Some look to the West Indies, and from that quarter they believe a large annual supply might be derived. The liberated negroes are willing to perform the work for a reasonable day's wage, and the quality of the cotton is good. Good; but we need a much larger supply than we are likely to receive permanently from Jamaica.'

Others direct their eye to India. There, it is alleged, that any quantity of the raw material may be produced. This we don't mean to dispute; but the question of production or growth is not the only one. In India, two difficulties meet us: first, the carriage of the cotton when produced, and the uncertainty of the allegiance of the Indian hordes. According to accounts, the difficulty and the expense of land carriage, before the cotton can be put on board ship, amount almost to a prohibition. And then it must be admitted that experience has taught us that little dependence is to be placed in a subject community like that of India.

The same or similar difficulties will meet us were we to turn our attention to Brazil, or to any other foreign country. We want to have the supply more steady than any half-civilized or subject people can ever secure to us; and we must have it, accompanied with fewer contingencies than we ever can expect to have, if the main sources of supply are in countries over which Britain has no control, or in which her authority may be disputed.

There are some persons who believe that England has no need, even in the matter of cotton, to lean upon others. We can conceive of circumstances in which a great nation like the English might be placed, and which, while they could not prevent such anxieties and inquiries as at present prevail, might yet effectually prevent the application of any remedial measure. She might have had no influence in the Indian Ocean, no access to the products of Hindostan; she might never have had, or, having them, might have been denuded of, her semi-tropical possessions in the Southern hemisphere; and situated so, however much she might have felt and deplored her dependence, from force of circumstances she must be dependent still.

But England is not so situated. Thanks to a beneficent Providence, she holds the remedy in her own hand; it remains to be proved whether she has the wisdom, and will have the patience and perseverance to apply it.

She may draw much more largely than she has ever done on her possessions, both in the East and the West Indies. From these sources united, a large proportion of the raw material might be realized under a properly organized system of cultivation, although it would be folly to depend upon them. In these countries, where the labour is cheap and abundant, and where the commonest kinds could be grown, a successful competition might be organized, and the American planter be made to feel that the slave-produced article was not so absolutely in possession of the market of the world as he fancied.

But, best of all, Britain possesses in her own loyal dependencies, in the Southern hemisphere, a vast extent of territory, which, both as it regards soil and climate for the growth of the plant, and the means of conveyance to the shipping in any of the ports over a sea-board of 600 miles, is unsurpassed in any country in the world. Providence seems to have destined the cotton-field of Queensland to be cultivated by British labour, and thus afford the most convincing of all proofs that our cotton supply is not dependent on slavery. Such a monstrous evil cannot much longer exist. The country where it is cherished will never be secure, and will never prosper; nor will the interests dependent upon it ever be secure against fluctuation and sudden change. Neither the North nor the South portion of the (United) States have apparently any serious intention of removing the evil. They are devotees of the "almighty dollar," and are not troubled with a scrupulous conscience. Britain has now the opportunity of showing them a better way. Were the view which we have ventured to take and express in these pages of our cotton supply in connexion with the extensive emigration of industrious families, to be countenanced by our manufacturers, merchants, and statesmen, ere long we should have on the sea-board of Queensland a large white population engaged in the profitable production of cotton, quite equal to the finest American fibres.

## XV.—QUEENSLAND COTTON-FIELD AND COTTON.

The reader will naturally desiderate some account of the proposed cotton-field in Queensland, and also of the cotton produced there. This we shall supply in the present chapter. As regards the quantity of land that might be put under cotton, that may be said to extend from the Logan, near the south boundary, along the coast for at least 600 miles, with an inland range of about 50 miles, including most of the islands that skirt the coast. It is, of course, impossible to place all this vast breadth of country under crop at once, even though we had the necessary white labour landed on its shores;

for it is more or less heavily timbered, and must first be cleared, and fitted for the plant. This is the work of time; but, in time, we doubt not, it will be accomplished. The districts that have been selected as agricultural reserves are not only of rich soil, but also, on the average, thinly timbered. Here, of course, the clearing commences, and from each centre it will gradually spread till the country shall be denuded of much of its robust vegetation. Inland, the cotton produced may not be so good in quality, and will, therefore, not be so high in price; but near the coast, and on the islands, any quantity of the cotton, known in the market as "Sea Island," may be produced. There is field enough here to grow as much as England at present consumes.

The excellence of the Queensland cotton-field does not altogether lie in its vast extent. The soil, although varied, is most admirably suited to produce crops of the finest quality; and because of the suitable soils being associated with a fine climate, the quantity corresponds with the quality. It will, therefore, pay the farmer to devote his capital and attention to its cultivation. This vast cotton-field, with a soil and climate so admirably adapted to the production of the finest fibre known in our home-market, has yet another important recommendation. Along the coast there are at least four harbours, where large ships may receive their cargoes—Brisbane, Marybourgh, Gladstone, and Rockhampton; and, ere long, ships drawing over 22 feet will be able to sail right up the river Brisbane, and anchor in the very heart of the capital. By this time the steam-dredge is at work to remove the few obstacles in the shape of sand and mud-banks. Add to this the fact, that a large portion of the richest lands on the coast is completely intersected by navigable streams and creeks for at least 15 miles inland, and you perceive how wonderfully favoured this colony is by a kind Providence. Besides all this, the climate is such that Europeans, with ordinary care, can do a regular and fair day's work, even in the hottest months, with impunity. I am aware that many persons think this impossible; and on this assumption they build one of their great arguments for coolie labour. But I have only to remind the reader of what is stated under the head "Climate" in an early part of this work, and to add that, every lawful day in the year, shepherds, bullock-drivers, masons, and the whole class of labourers, and small farmers, constantly ply their avocations with at least as little mortality as befalls the same classes at home.

Of Queensland cotton-field, this is the sum of what has been stated:—It is of vast extent, being 600 miles long by 50 wide, besides containing nearly all the islands on the coast. The soil varies, but is all admirably adapted to the growth of cotton in its best varieties, especially Sea Island. The climate is most favourable to the plant, and *not* inimical to the European constitution. White men labour all the year over, with no more disease, and no higher rate of mortality, than at home. There are numerous navigable streams and creeks ready prepared to convey the bales of cotton to the harbours, with which the coast is largely provided, thence to be wafted, along with wool and other products, direct to the ports of London, Liverpool, and Glasgow.

But some one may ask—"Has the cotton-producing power of Queensland ever really been tested? Has the plant been grown there, and has the fibre been examined, and spun, and converted into cloth? The most conclusive reasoning is not enough; the matter should be brought to experiment."

A reasonable question, and well put. I quite agree with you, that the matter is much too important to be placed on any ground short of experiment, and on this ground alone do we place it. I must, therefore, request your attention to the evidence of the superior quality of the limited quantities of cotton that have been grown in Queensland, and valued, and bought, and converted into cloth by English brokers and manufacturers.

In 1854, when Queensland was connected with New South Wales, a quantity of cotton grown there was submitted to Messrs. Hollingshead and Co., of Liverpool, for examination. The report of these gentlemen was in these terms:—"We have carefully examined the sample of Australian cotton sent us for valuation. It ranks with the highest class of Sea Island cotton, and, free from the few spots of stain, is worth 3s. per pound in this market. It is superior in fineness and evenness of staple, though a little inferior in strength of staple, as compared with Sea Island. We return you the sample, as you may not have retained any, and send you a small bit of Sea Island worth to-day 2s. 6d. per pound, and another purchased to-day at 2s. 9d., both inferior to your sample, in our opinion, and in the opinion of the buyer of the 2s. 9d. lot."

Three years later, that is, in 1857, Mr. Clegg, Manchester, addressed the following letter to Messrs. R. Barbour and Brothers, of the same city, which is too valuable in several respects to be curtailed:—"It gives me pleasure to state, after consulting Mr. Bazley, Messrs. Houldsworth, Barnes, and Co., and a dealer in Sea Island cotton, that the sample you sent to me is of very superior quality, almost too good for ordinary fine yarns and for practical purposes. It was variously valued at from 2s. to even 4s. per lb. for fancy articles, the prevailing opinion being that it would realize 2s. 6d. to 3s. per lb., which I believe it would for moderate quantities, but great quantities of such valuable sorts are not required, being of limited consumption. I think, however, they might fairly calculate upon 2s. per lb. for a long time to come for such cotton. I have no doubt that, where this was grown, they can produce, *in quantity*, the best cotton in the world perhaps, and ought forthwith to turn their attention to it, by getting abundance of labour either from China or from other sources, free from any risk of introducing slavery in its cultivation.

"Your friends are right in saying that great care will be required in cleaning the cotton, so as *not to damage its colour or injure the staple*. For this purpose, none but the roller gin should be used, unless, perhaps, M'Cartney's, which might also be tried, and both are made in Manchester at Messrs. Dunlop's; I can get them right for your friends' experiments if they wish. This fine cotton would, however, pay to be picked, sorted, and cleaned even by hand, although slow work.

"The seed should be *dry and hard* before being cleaned, otherwise it crushes instead of leaving the cotton freely, and the *oil* in the seed stains the cotton. The finest and best grown pods should always be kept together, the next ditto, and even a third quality of inferior ones; by these means the best prices would be realized for each, whereas, if mixed altogether, the whole would only sell for what the inferior alone would fetch.

"A gentleman who has a son in Australia has previously

sent me samples of this cotton, and they cannot do better than begin to plant all in their power, and send it in quantity. I shall have great pleasure in selling such as they may send, to enable them to get the best possible price for it. To show that there is no risk, I dare at this moment buy 500 bales, of from 300 to 500 lbs. each, of this, at 2s. per lb. Do not, however, let them deceive themselves, but calculate, as one of themselves lately said, on realizing an average of 1s. 3d. to 1s. 6d. per lb. Even this would be a very high price, Indian cotton ranging from 3d. to 5d.; American bowed uplands Orleans, $3\frac{1}{2}$d. to $8\frac{1}{2}$d.; Brazil, and similar staple, 5d. to 8d.; Egyptian, from $5\frac{1}{2}$d. to 10d.; and Sea Island (your variety), 11d. to 2s. fine quality to 4s. per lb."

In the close of 1859, Mr. Haywood, Secretary to the "Cotton Supply Association," Manchester, in a letter addressed to Sir William Denison, then Governor of New South Wales, thus expresses himself:—

"We are frequently receiving information of small parcels of most valuable cotton arriving from Australia, and there is a strong desire on the part of our spinners to obtain more. The class of cotton I refer to is a beautiful long staple cotton, of which I have received and sold parcels at 1s. 8d. to 2s. per lb. The demand for this class of cotton is limited, as compared with the New Orleans variety, but there is no doubt that all of the better class that is likely to arrive in this country for many years to come will be eagerly bought up, and I shall be happy to call public attention to any consignments of which I may be advised, and to find a market for it if consigned to this address."

At a meeting held in Manchester about two years ago, Mr. Bazley is reported to have addressed his audience in these terms regarding Queensland cotton and its cultivation:—

"About five years ago a few bags of Moreton Bay (Queensland) cotton were shipped to Liverpool, and I saw at once that, with such vastly superior cotton, yarn could be produced finer than any that could be manufactured in India or Great Britain. I bought that cotton, carried it to Manchester, and spun it into exquisitely fine yarn. I found that the weavers of Lancashire could not produce a fabric from it, it was so exceedingly delicate; the weavers of Scotland could not weave it; nor could even the manufacturers of France weave this yarn into fine muslin. It occurred to me to send it to Calcutta, and in due time I had the happiness of receiving from India some of the finest muslin ever manufactured, the produce of the skill of the Hindoos with this delicate Australian cotton. At the Paris Exhibition, some of this muslin was placed in the same glass case with a large golden nugget from Australia, and the two attracted much attention. The soil and climate of Queensland are capable of producing, with proper care, 600 lbs. yearly per acre of this exquisitely fine cotton. Two crops could be grown each year. I value this cotton at 1s. 3d. per lb., which would be equal to £40 per acre. This is no over estimate, for I have recently given 1s. 8d. per lb. for Australian cotton. Now, £40 per acre is an enormous yield for any agricultural product; and I do not think such a profitable return could be obtained in any other country. Judging by what is done in the United States, a man with his family in Queensland could cultivate ten acres of land, which would yield £400 per annum—a very high rate of profit."

Most readers would be satisfied with the evidence presented above in proof of the superior nature of Queensland cotton; but I have another witness whom I must produce. He is a gentleman still resident in the colony, and who has taken a lively interest in the subject of cotton growth for at least ten or twelve years. No man is better qualified than Dr. Hobbs, the gentleman to whom I now refer, to express an opinion on this subject. About five years ago, Mr. T. S. Mort, Sydney, who has always taken a lively interest in the subject, submitted certain queries to Dr. Hobbs, the replies to which were embodied in a paper which appeared in Cox & Co.'s Australian Almanac for 1857. I shall transcribe a few of these questions, with the replies which they elicited:—

"What species or varieties of cotton are cultivated, if any, in Moreton Bay (Queensland)?"

"The Sea Island, introduced into the district by S. A. Donaldson, Esq., Sydney (now in England), seven years ago, propagated and distributed by myself to most of the growers in the neighbourhood. A very superior description of Sea Island is being cultivated this season, propagated from seed introduced by Captain W. B. O'Connell, which he brought from the prize sample in the Great Exhibition in London in 1851."

"What variety is cultivated to the best advantage?"

"The Sea Island, decidedly. Several coarser varieties have been tried and found to answer well."

"How long have they been cultivated there, and from what country were they obtained?"

"Experimental patches for seven years. The seed imported from America."

"Has the general character of the cotton fibre, as to length, strength, or uniformity, deteriorated since its introduction?"

"No; the cotton from seed given by me to Mr. Eldridge has obtained prizes wherever exhibited—viz., a £30 prize three years ago at Sydney, a silver medal at the Sydney Exhibition, and another silver medal at the Paris Exhibition."

"What is the usual price of ginned cotton fibre per pound?"

"The cotton sent from here has been usually picked by hand; such samples have been valued at Manchester and Glasgow at 1s. 9d. to 2s. 6d. per pound."

"Are the soil and climate well adapted to its profitable growth?"

"Admirably adapted."

The cotton at present to be seen in the International Exhibition, from Queensland, and which has been valued by competent persons at 3s. 6d. per pound, bears out to the full, the strongest remark I have ventured to make regarding the staple grown in the new colony.

Queensland furnishes one of the most magnificent cotton-fields to be found in the world. The facts stated, the character of which you are capable of judging, justify me in making this unqualified statement. And the evidence which I have collected and embodied in these few pages demonstrates that in no other field is cotton of a superior character likely to be produced.

## XVI.—WHITE LABOUR, OR BLACK LABOUR, OR BOTH?

Just as certain as the question of cotton supply is one of vast importance to England at this time, and will continue to be, so certain is it that Queensland provides her with a magnificent cotton-field of her own, and that the cotton fibre produced there cannot be surpassed. What need, then, of further anxiety in this matter? Why such condolings because of the interruption in the American supply? Why not direct our labour, and skill, and capital to the genial southern hemisphere, and, with all the energy and indomitable perseverance of our race, produce our own raw material? No one can complain of this. I fancy we are as free to grow cotton as to manufacture it. And should the fact of our becoming our own producers offend brother Jonathan, and render his slave-produced cotton an unprofitable speculation, it really cannot be helped. In sober truth, whilst this is clearly the course on which England should now enter, it is the only way in which slavery is likely to be abolished. Render the "domestic institution" an unprofitable concern, and it will cease to be. This is an irresistible argument, and well will it be for America should the evil be removed thus.

"Good," says the intelligent reader; "it is most desirable that England should have her own cotton-field; it is plain that cotton, of a high character, can be produced in Queensland. But the question is, can *we* produce our own raw material, and, if we can, by what labour?

It is alleged, however, by some that it would be unwise to depend on Queensland as the source of our cotton supply in its more valuable varieties, because it is a country where the low and rich lands are subject to floods. In point of fact, the lands suited for the cultivation of cotton, sugar, &c., are not subject to floods; and when they do come, they are not so tremendous as they are represented to be by those who deal in the marvellous. A few years ago, there was a great flood in the Brisbane, its principal tributary, the Bremer, having risen some 40 feet. But this is altogether exceptional. The rivers in Queensland rarely rise to a height destructive of growing crops. It is further alleged that the season for picking the cotton is wet and unfavourable; and by a strange perversity, some even affirm that the seasons are too dry for the cultivation of this plant. The truth is, there are no very marked seasons of rain or drought there, but generally such a proportion of rain and sunshine as greatly contributes to the productiveness of the soil, and the beauty and healthfulness of the climate.

We admit that the labour question is the great question of the day. We have said as much already. It is not enough to show that our colony is capable of producing such and such staples in great demand at home or elsewhere; it must also be shown that they can be produced at remunerative prices, and by what kind of labour—white, or black, or both.

In England, and in the colony also, there is diversity of opinion on this question. In Queensland, there is *now* a strong party in favour of the introduction of Chinese and coolie labour; and with this party it is obvious that the majority of manufacturers and capitalists in this country who take any interest in this matter sympathize. The prominent members of this party, in their letters, and speeches, and communications to the public press, deal in very sweeping assertions. They allege that the cotton-field in Queensland can never, and will never, be cultivated unless by the introduction of thousands of coolies and Chinese. I am not surprised at such an assertion proceeding from a home orator, or appearing in a home newspaper article; for many of the data indispensable to an accurate judgment in the matter are cognizable only by those who have some colonial experience—experience, I mean, gained, not in the other colonies, but in Queensland itself. But it rather startles one to read the discussions that appear in the Queensland papers on this point. Without presuming to dogmatize, I shall state my own opinion; without anticipating the approbation of either party, I shall proceed to give as fair a view of the two sides of the case as I can, and suggest a course which might possibly add to the white labour production somewhat of profit, and take from the idea of coolie labour some of its offensiveness.

The advocates of coolie labour rest their case on two grounds. Other considerations may be, in some instances, added, but all may be substantially reduced to these two:—

1. *The price of labour.*—That white labour is high, is a fact that neither of the parties deny, and it is used by the advocates of colonization to induce the home population to proceed to the colony. It is alleged that cotton cannot be grown at this hour in Queensland, with wages at the present rates, by white

labour, at such a profit as would justify the employment of British capital. The only way this assertion can be met is by an appeal to statistics.

But, first, I shall place before the reader the results of two experiments made by Mr. Hill, the Director of the Botanical Gardens, Brisbane :—

"In the months of September, 1857 and 1858, a half an acre of ground on an open situation, of a sandy loamy soil, was selected and dug one spade deep for the cultivation of the Sea Island cotton plant. Previously to planting, the seeds were steeped in water during some hours; they were afterwards rolled in sand in order entirely to separate them from each other. This process very much accelerates their germination. In the month of October, the seeds were planted in rows, four feet distance from each other; two or three seeds were dropped in each hole, because some of them are liable to rot in the ground; the seeds were covered with earth one inch thick. The plants made their appearance in about eight days. At about the end of four weeks the ground was carefully weeded, and those plants which were the weakest were drawn, and only one plant left in the hole. The ground was frequently hoed and kept free from weeds. When the plants were about five months old, they showed signs of flowering. The stems and branches were thinned, and about an inch was broken off from the end of each shoot to determine the sap of the capsules. The time of the seeds coming to maturity was little more than six months after they had been planted. This period is, however, well indicated by the spontaneous bursting of the capsule, or seed pod. In gathering the fibre, care was taken to withdraw it from the capsule, leaving the empty husks upon the plant. This work was always performed as soon as possible after the fibre displayed itself, for long exposure to the sun injures its colour. The process of gathering lasts till the middle of July. The fibre and seeds of one hundred plants were kept separate in gathering each season. Each plant produced 11 ounces of seed and 4 ounces of fibre, yielding at the rate of 1,871 lbs. 6 ounces of seed, and 680 lbs. 8 ounces of fibre per acre. Samples of the fibre were forwarded to England with the view of testing its quality and value. The report received stated the fibre appeared to the eye to be of excellent quality, and its value would be from 2s. to 2s. 6d. per lb. in London. I may state the Sea Island cotton plant is a perennial here, and improves in quantity and quality for two or three years, after which period it will be liable to degenerate. I may also mention that this plant is of easy cultivation, and quite within the scope of any ordinary man's ability who can use a spade or hoe. The most important operation is the picking of the fibre, as the pods ripen and open out, and that can be easily performed by the younger branches of a man's family."

The above extract has special reference to Brisbane and its neighbourhood, and merits the full confidence of the reader. Some extracts that will appear in a future chapter, from Mr. Sloman's pamphlet, have special reference to the country about Rockhampton. Mr. Hill estimates the crop of Sea Island per acre at 600 lbs. clean cotton (we take it 400 lbs.); Mr. Bazley estimates the value at not less than 1s. 4d. per lb.; freight to England 1d. per lb.; the real value of Queensland Sea Island cotton, therefore, may be said to be 1s. 3d. per lb. Mr. Mann, in his "Cotton Trade of Great Britain," calculates that a man and a boy may cultivate 10 acres. Let us suppose a company, with a capital of £10,000, started to grow cotton by British labour. The number of families required would be 40, with an average of four adults, *i.e.* three adults and two children. The first year only a portion of the land which the 40 families could cultivate would be ready, and even the cotton would not be in such quantity as in succeeding seasons. The grants of land, equal to the cost of the passage-money, constitute a valuable freehold property.

### FIRST YEAR.

| Outlay— | £ | Returns— | £ |
|---|---|---|---|
| Passage, 40 families, at £18 per adult | 2,880 | Land Grants equal to | 2,880 |
| Passage, 2 Superintendents | 100 | Say 200 bales of 300 lbs., at 1s. 3d. per lb. | 3,750 |
| Bullocks, horses, drays, implements | 500 | Government Bonus as a Premium for production for 3 years in Land Orders, value 8d. per lb. (to be continued for half the amount for the 2 succeeding years) | 2,000 |
| Extras | 400 | | |
| | £3,880 | Other products, corn, potatoes, arrowroot, &c. | 500 |
| *Expenses—* | | | £9,130 |
| Wages, 40 men, at £40; 40 boys at £20 | 2,400 | | |
| Rations, 2 to each family, at 8s. per week | 1,664 | | |
| Two Superintendents | 700 | | |
| Packs and Extras | 440 | | |
| Interest on outlay, at 10 per cent. | 388 | | |
| | 5,592 | | |
| | £9,472 | | |

## SECOND YEAR.

| | | | |
|---|---|---|---|
| Working Expenses, wear and tear | £5,700 | Cotton, 400 bales, at 1s. 3d. per lb. | £7,500 |
| Interest | 388 | Government Bonus | 4,000 |
| | £6,088 | Other products | 1,000 |
| | | | £12,500 |

## THIRD YEAR.

| | | | |
|---|---|---|---|
| Working Expenses, wear and tear | £5,800 | Cotton, 500 bales | £9,375 |
| Interest | 388 | Government Bonus | 5,000 |
| | £6,188 | Other products | 1,000 |
| | | | £15,375 |

It is quite possible that the returns the first year may not be so great, although we have proceeded on the calculations made by gentlemen resident in the colony, and were we to deduct from the returns 25 per cent., still the company would be in a very prosperous condition. The fourth year the Government bonus would be very much reduced, and in a year or two more it would cease to be granted; but in the meantime the breadth of cotton planted is increasing, and its quality improving, and thus the difference is made up in the most legitimate way. We cannot, therefore, admit the assertion that cotton cannot be grown in Queensland by white labour, and that, therefore, British capitalists will not be induced to enter the field unless coolie labour is employed. Where would the capitalist meet with such a per centage for his money, on the double guarantee of the value of the land in the colony, and the steady demand for the cotton fibre in England? I have based these calculations on the minimum results that have been obtained by those who have experimented in the matter of cotton-growth, being desirous that the cultivator should find his returns not worse, but better, than I have calculated them.

It is alleged by some that as there is but a limited demand for Sea Island cotton, were Queensland cotton-field to be largely cultivated, the price must of necessity decline. It is by no means certain that this result would follow; but if it should, the cultivation of the cotton plant would still be one of the most profitable occupations in Queensland, and worthy of the serious attention of British capitalists.

2. The second ground on which coolie labour is asserted to be the only labour that can ever be permanently employed in Queensland, in the production of cotton and kindred articles, is *the climate.* It is alleged that the climate of that colony is

so hot and so hurtful to European health, that it will be a failure, on this ground, were there no other reason against it, to employ white labour. Parties at home may reason themselves into this belief, and parties in the colony may find it convenient to use this argument; but no man who has been there, and who has taken note of what passes every day, will attempt to refute the statements I have made in previous parts of this work regarding the healthiness of the climate, and the impunity with which white men work in the open air, keeping free from strong drink and not unnecessarily exposing themselves. Besides, the principal work, the work of picking, is performed in the months of "May, June, and July, when the climate is eminently serene and salubrious."

There are several occupations in which many white men are engaged, and which must be carried on in all weathers and in all seasons. I shall, at present, pass by the numerous hands, amounting to several thousands, who are engaged all the days in the year, in the open air, on stations. Very often this class of persons are regardless of their comfort and health by taking drink to excess whenever they can get it, and in many instances their health was seriously injured before they went on stations at all, and thus bad health is brought on, and death follows; but, after all, the mortality among them is not high. All the men who are engaged in such occupations as that of the mason, the joiner, the road-maker, the land-clearer, the shingle-splitter, the fencer, the wood-cutter, the gardener, the farmer, are exposed to the sun all the year round. No one will venture to affirm that, when these men observe temperate habits, there is more mortality among them than among others whose avocations keep them under shelter. And no one up to this moment has ventured to suggest that the climate is too hot for these men, and that, therefore, if their work is to be done at all, it must be done by Chinese or coolies. Why is the white man able to do all other kinds of work in the open air, except the cultivation of cotton? How is it that the European plants, and hoes, and hills maize and potatoes in one part of his farm with impunity, while he exposes himself to injury, perhaps to sunstroke, should he attempt the cultivation of cotton on some other part? No one can explain this inconsistency. There are, every day in the year, 20,000 white persons in Queensland more or less exposed to the sun, and yet the mortality is lower than in England.

The truth of the matter is this—the climate of the southern portion (for it is of it we are speaking) of Queensland is warm but it is not injurious to European constitutions; men, in thousands, are working all day, and all lawful days of the year, at all kinds of out-door occupations; and thousands more might be employed on cotton farms with impunity. Several other occupations that must be carried on, and are always carried on by white labour, such as road-making, fencing, and farming, are much more laborious than cotton cultivation.

We must hold, therefore, that cotton may at this moment be cultivated in Queensland, in large well-conducted farms, by white labour, at a profit amply sufficient to encourage the investment of capital. Neither the climate, nor the high price of European labour, necessitates the employment of Chinese or coolies.

To develop the resources of the country, you may establish large farms or plantations; and, in this case, you must have a large capital, joint-stock or otherwise, to purchase land, to clear and stump it, to till, and to put it under crop; but you may be sure that the proper management of your plantation will result in a very good return for your money. Thirty per cent. is not to be got every day, nor is it to be got in every country. Or you may parcel the country into small farms of from 30 to 80 acres, and put down one or two industrious families on each. In this case, comparatively little money is required; for the head to plan, the hand to work, and the determination to "get on," constitute the most desirable capital. There is no antagonism between the capitalist and the small farmer; both can work together; there is "scope and verge enough" for all, and they will speedily become helps to each other.

On several grounds I should rejoice to see thousands of industrious families of the last-named class settling on all the agricultural reserves in Queensland; and this, were men to study their own and their families' interests, will soon be realized. They will do admirably as cotton farmers, as I shall show in a future chapter. But we must say that we believe that the prosperity of the colony would progress the more satisfactorily, were the capitalist also to enter the field in right good earnest. It will be seen that our opinion is, that the first consideration of the colonial Government should be to stimulate emigration of the right class to the shores of Queensland, and by every facility to encourage its settlement on the good agricultural lands. And this the Government is at present doing by means of the appointment of a Commissioner, who is now in England, by means of free grants of land of 30 acres to every emigrant, man or woman, who shall pay their passage-money, or get their friends to do it for them, and by giving the parties when they reach their choice of their lots from thousands of acres of the best soil in the colony.

At this stage I may be permitted to say a word or two in support of these views. Should we not have a care over those numerous families that abound in all parts of our country, who have the sorest struggle to keep out of debt and out of the workhouse, and who are well fitted, both from character and from previous occupation, to become the successful cultivators of the soil in such a colony as Queensland? Besides, there are many families who make a tolerable living here, but who, for reasons of their own, have the wish to transfer themselves to a new soil, where they may have a better chance of the prizes in the race of life. It is a first duty, alike with the home and colonial statesman, to facilitate the emigration of such families to a country so capable of yielding them ample support, and where they may have the widest and freest scope for their energies.

If we wish a colony to begin well and make steady progress in its moral and material developments, give as many as possible an interest in the soil. Get them to possess themselves of land. They may not all go into agriculture—that is not desirable; they may not, therefore, all till the soil; but whether they till it, live on it, or let it, let them have some land in freehold. It would be good policy in the Government to give the people land, rather than that they should be without it. When the body of the people in a new country are proprietors of land, you have a guarantee at once for the surest material development, and for the largest amount of social order.

The labour of the small proprietors is more productive than hired labour, either black or white. This question cannot be determined by statistics, although those who discuss it generally hedge themselves round with a formidable array of figures. When you have got an accurate statement of the relative number of hours per week the respective parties are engaged, and the relative sums paid for labour and rations, the real question is often not touched. There are so many subtle influences at work. Every one knows that hired labour and proprietary labour, that is, labour for one's own interest, differ somewhat in character and productiveness at home, and the difference is not lessened in colonies. Of the principle we say nothing; it is the fact we note. If the difference be palpable between the labour of white men, according as it may be hired or proprietary, the difference both in quantity and quality between the labour of the white proprietor and that of the hired coolie is alarmingly great. This alone, in our judgment, places the small farmer cultivating his own farm on at least equal ground, relative to proportionate returns, with the capitalist who works his plantation by coolie labour.

Those who have raised the cry for coolie labour seem to us to have overlooked several things in their calculations which have a serious bearing on the results. They imagine that coolie labour will be as cheap to the Queensland importer as it is to the West India planter, forgetting that while in the one case the competition is with liberated slaves, in the other it is with free men, each living and labouring on his freehold property. This must, in the nature of things, make a palpable difference. Nor is this all. It would be peculiarly difficult to enforce conditions of engagement entered into between agents and coolies in a foreign country, when the latter found themselves breathing an atmosphere of freedom, and perhaps might have grounds to suspect that when the bargain was struck between them and their employers, the truth was not all told them, or if told, not understood. Besides, it must be considered that there are coolies in the colony who make engagements, and even undertake piecework, on their own account, and who earn wages little lower than the white man. Is it to be doubted that the influence of these naturalized coolies will be exerted to secure for their sable brothers that arrangements shall be as favourable as possible? The chief object of the importer is to secure cheap labour; the coolie will undoubtedly help his race to secure a "fair day's wage for a fair day's work." Even tho dull and dreamy darkie learns to comprehend this righteous principle.

We have paid some attention to the question of coolie labour; we have seen both Indians and Chinese at work; we have visited many farms, the freehold property of their cultivators, and marked what was done, and what with moderate enterprise might be done; we have weighed with as little prejudice as possible the question of black *versus* white labour, as it bears on Queensland, the colony with which we are best acquainted; and the conclusion to which we have been brought is this—that should the colonial Government, by wise legislation and honourable inducements, attract the proper style of emigrants to the colony, and place them on easy terms on their own freehold farms, British labour, skill, and energy will prove themselves equal in productiveness to any coloured labour which it is possible to obtain.

Such are the views I have been led to entertain regarding the question of white labour or black labour for the new colony; and as the grounds on which my opinions rest have been placed before the reader, he is invited to examine them and judge for himself.

But strongly as I hold by these views, I have no well-grounded objection to urge against the incoming of coolies and Chinese to the colony in accordance with established law. Whilst we would not have Government by any legislative act to bring them in, neither would we wish Government by any legislative act to keep them out. And this is the law upon the subject:—Government does not undertake to introduce either coolies or Chinese into the colony; but neither does it put any obstacle in the way of those employers who desire to make a trial of that kind of labour. This is precisely as it should be. But it is proper that the reader should be apprized that the system of "engagements," whether made in Europe or in Asia, to serve masters in the colonies on conditions which the contracting party cannot possibly understand, never works well; it is vicious in principle and mischievous in practice. A man may with perfect safety engage, through an authorized agent, to serve any master who may be disposed to advance the money for his passage; but whilst he pledges himself to enter and continue in that gentleman's employment, the terms ought to be at the current wages. Never fix wages till your arrival, and then accept what is currently given.

In accordance with these views I am prepared to admit, that, whilst I believe that an influx of many thousands of coolies into Queensland in present circumstances would not contribute so much to its prosperity as most of the advocates of that system imagine, yet, so far as I can judge, a proportion of coolie labour might be advantageously employed along with the white. I can understand, for example, how the small proprietor, whose farm increases in its cotton-bearing proportions every year, might find room for one or two black servants, and, by his constant presence and daily example, teach them to do work according to his plans. But, as the rule, at least for the time, I would have black labour merely as an adjunct to the white, not as the mainstay of the farm. These are the views which I have been led to adopt on the question of labour in Queensland at the present time; what may be wisest and best in the future is a question which should always be left open, when it refers to new countries. My objection to coolie labour is not so much on principle as on expediency; and, so far as I can judge, I believe the best thing for that colony at its present stage is a large influx of well-principled and industrious families from home. In this way alone will you lay the foundation of a large and prosperous community worthy of the name of Britain.

## XVII.—OUR COTTON FARM.

Some years ago several parties possessed of land experimented on cotton, and found it do very well. Various causes contributed to diminish the interest felt in this staple for a time in Queensland. These need not be enumerated here, as they had no bearing whatever on its productiveness. The interest has been revived in the colony as well as in home circles, and this time it is placed under more favourable auspices. There is the pressure of demand coming from England; and there is, in the colony itself, all that a Government can legitimately do to stimulate and to encourage. The "free grants" of land and the "bonus" are very great encouragements; and this kind of help or stimulus is not to be viewed in the light of "protection." The "bonus," at the rate of 8d. per lb. of clean cotton, is the encouragement given for a time to the farmer who is already in possession of his land in freehold; the double inducement of 30 acres to each emigrant who pays his passage out, and also the "bonus," is held out to all deserving men who may be thinking of leaving their own country. The grants of land themselves are a perfect fortune to a working man with a wife and family; for, if in any honourable way he can manage to pay his passage out, he may have from 60 to 120 acres of land capable of growing any kind of crops which he may wish to cultivate.

I shall take a case, which, when emigration has steadily set in, will not be a rare one. I shall take a man with a wife and two children above four but under fourteen years of age. According to the Government regulations in force in Queensland, this man, by paying three adult passages, receives in land orders 90 acres. But you will observe, in the first place, that the sum required for the passage will be three times £18, the passage-money for an adult, that is, £54. Now, few working men can command such a sum as this readily. We may suppose, however, that many may be able to realize £18 on their furniture, &c., from friends they may be able to borrow another £18, and many masters in Queensland may be induced to advance the £18 for the man, on condition that he engage to work for him at current wages for one year. The master has the land order for security, and the servant has the opportunity of redeeming it at its value, £18. The redemption of the land order is easy in the case of a well-doing man, in this way:—His wife and himself may be engaged by the same master; in that case the united wages will be, say about £50, and rations and house for the whole family for the year. By the end of that period, there being almost no expenditure, the man goes to his master, and addresses him thus:—

"Sir, you were kind enough to pay £18 of the passage-money for myself and family, on the condition that I should work for you at current wages for one year. You received one of my land orders of the value of £18, as security for the sum you paid. The period is now near a close, and when you settle with me, I desire, instead of the £50 money, the land order and the balance. I am much obliged to you for the part you have performed in my emigration, but now I desire a change."

"A change," says the master; "do you, then, think so lightly of what I have done, that at the very first opportunity you leave me, and engage in the service of another? This is poor encouragement for masters to take all the trouble of getting good workmen from home. Reconsider your decision."

"Sir, you entirely misunderstand me. I have no intention of engaging with another master; I may indeed take an occasional day's work, but that will be all. I assure you that I feel grateful for what you have done; but you are aware that my intention in coming to Queensland was to enter on the cultivation of cotton, and now I fancy myself in a position to commence. I have got accustomed to the climate a little; my wife and boys are eager for a little home of our own, and I am nothing loath, seeing I have got the balance of the year's wages to begin with."

"Ah! I see; very right; very right, very sorry to part with you though. But, really, do you intend to attempt the cultivation of cotton on such a slender capital?"

"Well, sir, I know of more than a dozen who reached the colony a year before us, who have been 12 months at the work, and declare that they dare not complain. You see, the wife and children help, and the work goes on cheerily. And I don't see as my good woman is not as fit to help me as any one I knows."

"All right; but, mind, if any difficulty should arise, you know where a letter will find me."

"Thank you, sir."

Our cotton grower had safely deposited the other two land orders in the bottom of the strong wooden box that contains all their valuables, and the third one is now added to the number. Of the 90 acres of land, the three orders he has will purchase 54; the other 36 will be in his possession at the end of the second year after his arrival.

Away he goes, then, with his three "orders" in his pocket, to the survey office. He examines the plans very carefully; but last week he spent a whole day in examining the reserve itself, on which he has resolved to settle. He selects 54 acres of the best land, conveniently situated for the carriage of the farm products, and places on the table as payment his three land orders. The clerk gives him in exchange a document signed and sealed, for which he pays one guinea; and now he is absolute proprietor of the farm of 54 acres.

He deposits the deeds in the strong box, and counts his money. After several items are deducted, he finds that the sum total of his capital is £27 10s. In addition, there are a mare and two cows bought by the small earnings of the two boys during the year. The eldest boy is now 15, and can take part with his father, and the youngest is a little behind him. From an old friend, who has been several years in the colony, and has got on well, an old cart is borrowed. The family, having laid in rations for three months, and various odds and ends, that have lessened their small capital by the sum of £6 10s., now start on their journey to "Our Farm." Observe this—they have in money £21, most of which they have put in the bank, as they wont need it in the bush till seed time, or when the supply of rations becomes low; they have one mare and two cows, 54 acres of good land near a navigable creek, and they have stout hearts, cool heads, and willing hands.

They have reached their farm, selected a site for the family dwelling, and cut down the first tree. A small wooden hut is soon raised, which will give place, by and bye, to one more substantial and attractive. Most of the articles of furniture, at the first offset, are made by the willing hands of the father and sons, and the strong box supplies the place of table. This arrangement I have seen in many instances; and in a country like Queensland, one feels it to be no serious drawback for a year or two. In a few days the trees, over an acre of ground, are cut down about three feet from the surface, and, green though they be, delivered over to the flames. The boys do a great part of the burning; and as the fires do their work of consuming the superfluous timber, the father, assisted at intervals by the boys, turns up the fine virgin soil around the stumps, drops a few potato seeds, plants a few sweet potato-vines, several rows of maize, a dozen grape-vines, and a double number of pine-apple and banana suckers, all of which they brought with them in the cart. In three months there will be a crop of maize, in a short time after potatoes, and fruit about this time next year.

The time the first planted crops are growing, all hands are at the felling of trees, the extracting of roots, the burning of the accumulating timber, and the erecting of a fence, made of the split timber. In three months two acres are ready to receive the cotton seed; and in 12 months the farmer takes the product of these two acres to the capital in the old cart, sells it, unginned as it is, to one of the shipping merchants, and receives for the crop, inferior the first year, the sum of £18. By hard labour during the year, other four acres have been prepared for cotton, as well as a good supply of maize, and potatoes, and green crop, produced for support of the family, and the nourishment of sundry pigs, and a sprinkling of poultry. The mare, too, has got a foal at her foot, and the cows are attracted homewards at sun-down by their calves that have been kept in the stock-yard all day to prevent the young thieves from draining the much-coveted milk. At this stage we may take stock, and ascertain how matters stand :—Money, very low; one mare and foal; two cows and two calves; four pigs; fourteen hens; nine turkeys; one acre under vegetables and fruit; six acres under cotton crop, at all events the plants on two are entering on their second year, and the seed on the other four is in the ground. A succession of vegetables is kept up, and as the bacon-cask looks low, another pig is given to the knife. There is a steady supply nearly all the year over of eggs, and milk, and butter, and fruit; and when the bacon becomes stale or monotonous, it is enlivened by the fattest fowl from the yard. Such is the material "condition" of our cotton grower at the commencement of his second year.

I have met with a small publication by H. J. Sloman, on the cultivation of the cotton plant in Australia, and from it I give the following extract, full of minute details of great practical value to the growers about Rockhampton :—

"When the ground is fenced, take a good heavy sharp hoe, about six inches in breadth, and cut off all the grass clean, and deep enough to kill all the roots; after which the grass and all other rubbish should be burnt. Then take a grubbing hoe, which ought to be four inches wide, and break up the ground fine, and fully a foot deep, taking care to cut everything that comes in the way of the hoe. Should the season be late, say October, plant the ground with maize, for October would be too late for cotton, and a maize crop would do the ground good, as it would cause it to get an extra turning. When the cotton is gathered in March, break up the ground fine, nine or ten inches deep, and draw it into ridges of six feet wide, taking care to make suitable cross-ditches so arranged as to carry off the water during heavy rains, or retain it when the retention of it would be beneficial to the crop. In April, should there be any rain, plant the cotton seed in the centre of each ridge, and should the seed be fresh and good, it will all grow. Plant three seeds in a triangle of about six inches, and let every triangle be six feet apart. Do not put the seeds in the ground more than one inch. Should the ground be moist and warm, the plant will be up in a week; but should any of the seeds fail to vegetate, then fill up the vacancies with more seed. The adoption of this method precludes the necessity of destroying any of the plants. By planting in April, the plants will be strong, and pod early, and hence the planter will be able to begin to pick in November. The seed may be planted during any month in the year when there is rain, or when the ground is in a moist state; but April, May, June, July, August, and September are the proper planting months. When the cotton is planted during the latter month, a crop of corn may be grown between the cotton plants, as they will not require all the ground that year, on account of having been planted late; but should the season be very favourable, that is, should there be abundance of rain, the cotton trees will require all the ground before the corn could be got off, and therefore it would be useless to plant the latter; but on this head experience will soon teach the planter when he should sow corn and when he should not. The cotton trees should always be kept clear and free from grass, and, in effecting this, the hoe should be used freely.

"Failures and accidents occur sometimes in cotton planting as well as in other pursuits. The trees often fail, owing to various causes. Some fail because they are overgrown by adjacent plants, and others in consequence of the continuance of dry weather. The planter must do his best to remedy all these failures, and then he may be sure that he will have a good standing field at the end of the third year, notwithstanding that he may have picked three good crops. A good average crop is 1,600 lbs. of cotton in the seed per acre, which will yield 400 lbs. of clear lint, or one bale, worth always not less than £30 sterling.

"Now, one able-bodied and industrious man could do a great deal more than merely cultivate six acres of cotton. If he were a married man, and had a family of four or five children to assist him, he could grow corn, potatoes, vegetables, as well as attend to many other things, besides cultivating a cotton crop; so that no horticultural or agricultural pursuit could be more profitable than that of cotton planting."

An able-bodied man and his family may cultivate successfully 10 acres of cotton, besides attending to other duties on the farm. On the management of the trees, the same writer makes some admirable remarks, and gives such directions as should be observed by all cotton farmers. The cotton plant in Queensland is not an annual as in America, but is a perennial, that with proper treatment may last and produce cotton during several years. Dr. Hobbs states that he had cotton on the same plants five years in succession, and the fifth year it was the finest. This is the extract on the management of the cotton plant:—

"When any of the trees fail, they should be cut off to the ground, or even under it, and young and vigorous plants transplanted in their place. The young trees should be transplanted before they have borne cotton or even come into blossom, and should the weather be dry, they must be kept well watered until they have taken root and are out of danger. Whole fields may be covered with a cotton crop by transplanting the young plants, provided there be long continued wet weather, or the planter should have the means of irrigation at hand. Whether the moisture be procured from natural or artificial sources, the plants must be watered for a sufficient length of time after being transplanted, for were not this done, the crop would fail; should the spring prove dry, the trees will be backward, and should the year be dry throughout, the growth will be exceedingly small; but should there be an abundance of rain in the months of October and November, the planter may be sure of having plants of wood, and, as a necessary corollary, plants of good cotton. The cotton should be gathered as soon as the pods open, or otherwise the cotton bugs would injure it by eating the staple asunder. As soon as their bearing shoots have made all their pods, and the lower ones are picked, all the main branches will throw out. The bearing branches will begin, should the weather prove favourable, to make the second set of branches from the same eyes, and close alongside of the first bearing branches, which will be ready for picking in April; so that, should there be a good year, the planter will have two full crops. As the picking proceeds, it is necessary that the plants should be pruned, as the dead leaves get in the way and stain the cotton. The picking will be finished at the end of July, for the cotton becomes poor and dull at that time, and the trees also must then be pruned thoroughly, in order to insure the next summer crop. At this time the ground should be hoed up, and all rubbish carried off, which will complete the out-door operations of the first year. There will now be plenty of time to gin the cotton, pack it off to market, and plant any other things that may be required.

"The six acres of ground now planted with cotton may receive a good dressing from the hoe. This can be readily effected, because, in consequence of the ground having been broken up a foot deep at first, the top root throws out its main side roots a good depth from the surface, and therefore the hoeing may be from two to three inches deep without doing any mischief. It is well, at the end of each year, to hoe down the ridges, and let the ground lie loose for a while, taking care to hoe in the dead leaves, which will serve as a manure for the trees.

"Before the young shoots grow too much, all the ridges should be raked up properly, and all the water-courses cleared out and the ground cleared, as the young shoots are very tender, and liable to be broken by people working amongst them. Let not the planter suppose that the trees are overgrown when they lie upon the ground, inasmuch as that is an effect produced by the branches being slender and the pods heavy. The cotton should be kept well picked, as in wet seasons, unless well looked after, it will begin to grow in the pods. Remember that during the first year the trees are not to be cut down or topped, but merely pruned, all the main branches being left standing."

The grower should carefully follow the directions given in this extract:—

"When the weather is very dry and the cotton opens quick, and the seeds are hard, the cotton should not be exposed on the frame for sunning as at other times. The cotton during such weather should be left in a cool place in heaps for a week, at the expiration of which time it will be found to have grown all out of the seed, and to have all the yolk in it, as should be the case with fully-matured cotton. If the cotton be really good, it will have a blueish yellowish soft colour, and feel firm, lively, and full in the hand, just the same as good fine wool would do; and this is what is meant by the phrase—'feeling the yolk in it.' The greatest care should be taken not to sweat the cotton, as sweating causes it to lose all its beauty and value.

"I have three sorts of fine cotton, about equal in value, and I let them grow together; but if I could procure sufficient labour, I would grow them separately. There are about 4,400 of my seeds to the pound weight, and I think 4,900 yards of ground to the acre; so that planting the seeds in the manner pointed out would give about 3,675 trees to the acre. It is a very poor season, indeed, if every tree does not yield $\frac{3}{4}$ lb. of cotton, so that the average value of the yield from an acre is very easily estimated. One of my sorts, and that, too, the best, will not admit of being planted so close as the other sorts of cotton. Half a pound of the seed of this will plant an acre."

The paragraph that follows has special reference to the treatment of trees in their second year:—

"Should the season prove favourable, the picking will be from the trees doubly grown, and covering the ground all over, and the knife must be freely used, inasmuch as, should it not be so used, half the crop will not be gathered. There will be plenty of work this year, from the beginning of December until the end of July, that being the end of the cotton year. At that time there will be plenty of cotton on, and pods not open, but this must be disregarded, in order to insure the health and pod-bearing ability of the trees. The trees will at this time be very large, and will comprise not only a main stem, but very many stems besides, and many young shoots still coming out, and the planter will, therefore, cut away one tree and leave one growing; that is to say, he will cut away the main stem at about two feet and a half from the ground, and all the large branches at about three inches to a foot, leaving two or three eyes between the part where the branch is cut and the main trunk or stem. Let all the young green branches that have never flowered remain on the tree, but cut off all that have pods on them, and that seem likely to open soon, for all such pods at this season do not open, but only make what is technically called 'feints.' As the season is ended, carry off all rubbish, hoe the ground deep, and, if possible, let it have a good soaking before the ridges are drawn up. This is the proper method of cultivating cotton in North Australia, within the tropic of Capricorn, on the sea coast, or as far inland as the sea breeze affects it."

This chapter has been written with facts and cases in my mind on which the various parts of it are founded; and as we have intentionally made our calculations on the safest data, the reader may receive the conclusions with confidence. I am aware that a specially unfavourable season, or the indolence or incapacity of the farmer, might bring about a very different result from the one given here; but all that can be reasonably expected that I should prove is this—that, in an average season, and when men understand their work, and perform it in season, the result will be most satisfactory. In such a case as I have supposed, the clear profits of the farm of 54 acres, 10 of which are under cotton, and one under vegetables, maize, and fruit, will be at the least £200 the second year. But, inasmuch as the cost of labour is not paid to strangers, but is reckoned to the farmer and his family, and growing such a quantity, he is entitled to the Government "bonus" also, the income of such a family, the second year, would be upwards of £300, reckoning the product of each acre at £25, which is a very fair figure, and almost the entire keep of the family besides, from the vegetables, poultry, pigs, and cows which he rears. And, in succeeding years, the cotton-producing capabilities of the farm might be increased to any extent by the use of white or black labour. Besides, at the close of the second year of his residence in the colony, the first of his residence on the farm, he receives the remainder of the "free

I

grants," 36 acres; and, year by year, his stock of cows and horses increases at a very high ratio—when well taken care of, at the rate of 70 per cent. per annum.

This is the prize which the Government of Queensland places within the reach of every industrious family in these islands; wise men, and men of energy, it is for you to consider what is to be done. All emigration should be voluntary; but sure we are, there does not exist in any part of the world a field more inviting, and more certain to reward you in a liberal manner, than the cotton-growing districts of Queensland. And you need not be, in the least degree, disconcerted by any remark that may be made in your hearing regarding the difficulty of cotton cultivation. It is, in truth, one of the easiest plants to grow; and, by following such directions as we have given, and others that are supplied in the colony for the use of beginners, you will find that no agricultural production can be undertaken with more certainty of success. I only desire that all those industrious families who have such struggles here to gain an honest living, were safely settled, each on their own Queensland Cotton Farm.

## XVIII.—SUGAR, FLAX, FRUITS, AND OTHER PRODUCTS.

A large portion of the colony is capable of growing sugar as well as cotton; and the capital and enterprise of Britain will certainly, in time, develop the one staple as well as the other to such an extent, at all events, as will supply the colonial wants. I have seen the sugar plants growing in several parts of the colony in great luxuriance, and have been informed by men who have had many years' experience on sugar plantations in the West Indies and elsewhere, that very much of the land by the banks of the Queensland rivers is capable of growing the sugar-cane and saccharine grasses to the greatest perfection.

I shall make an extract from a valuable paper, read before the Australian Horticultural and Agricultural Society, Sydney, by Dr. Günst, Richmond River, on the cultivation of the Sorghum Saccharatum, a Chinese sugar-grass or cane, that has been introduced into the Australian colonies within the last few years. This plant is of value in several respects, as the reader will perceive, and is likely to prove of great practical importance to the colonists:—" The Sorghum is a peculiar plant, and is valuable for many different qualities. Under skilful management, I have known it to produce no less than three crops in the course of the year. In spite of wind, weather, or drought, it will yield abundantly; for if the season be unfavourable for ripening the seed, we have an excellent crop of green fodder, which is eaten with avidity by all kinds of stock, including pigs; and by cutting the canes at the end of four months, you may always depend on another crop within four months afterwards. I can also assert that it will cost less to cultivate 100 acres of the Sorghum than 100 acres of wheat, while the yield is immeasurably more valuable. We commonly obtain two crops per annum, from which sugar may be extracted, and one crop of fodder. In order to estimate its superiority to wheat, let us suppose that it cost the same in the first instance to place 100 acres under cultivation as wheat, as it does to cultivate the same amount of Sorghum, we must then recollect that on an average we can only have one crop of wheat during the year, and that the produce per acre will be about 25 bushels. Let this be valued at the highest market price, and add to it the value of the straw, and that concludes the advantage derivable from it. For another crop, fresh seed, fresh ploughing and sowing is necessary; whereas in Sorghum, the plant once stuck in the ground goes on producing a crop for the year round, and is not attacked by drought, nor damaged with excessive wet, to the same extent as the cereal crops. If, after planting the Sorghum, we find that during the first two months of its growth the weather has been too wet, and we must abandon the hope of getting our crop of sugar—for the cane might not then yield sufficient saccharine matter—there will be sufficient to distil a spirit from the juice of the cane; and even if there were not enough of that, we would make vinegar, for even with inferior canes, I calculate that the acre of canes will produce 3,000 gallons of vinegar, besides having the seed, the leaves, and the refuse on which to feed the cattle. This we will suppose to be the result of the first four months' growth under unfavourable and wet weather. Within four months after this, if the weather is warm and favourable, we may have a fresh stock of canes, from which we may extract a crop of sugar, or even if the year throughout was wet and disastrous to all other cereal plants, we should, in the Sorghum, have an excellent stock of fodder. In the practice of my profession, as a medical man, stationed on the Richmond River, I have had many opportunities of observing the growth of the plant under very various circumstances in different localities, and thus I am enabled to speak so confidently of its value."

Dr. Günst has made, over a series of years, many experiments in the production of sugar from this plant. The results have been from time to time published in the colonial papers, and appear the most satisfactory that the farmer could desire. Richmond adjoins Queensland on the south, and the soil on the Logan, the Brisbane, and the Mary is equally well adapted to the successful growth of the Sorghum Saccharatum as that on the Richmond. In the Botanical Gardens at Brisbane, and on many farms, it has been grown with results quite equal to those arrived by Dr. Günst. This plant requires only four months to arrive at complete maturity; and in Queensland, Dr. Günst says, "We may safely reckon on three crops of sugar per annum." Sir William Macarthur, of Camden, Sydney, makes the following remarks regarding the cultivation of the sugarcane :—"There can be no question, I think, that with sufficient capital and an efficient management, the cultivation of the cane for sugar ought to prove one of the most profitable pursuits which offer themselves in Australia. I mean at Marybourgh or other places equally well situated on the north-east coast. I have for many years thought that sugar plantations to the northward of Moreton Bay ought to be highly remunerative. The climate is favourable, there is no lack of good land, and, unlike the Mauritius, we never hear of the ravages of hurricanes."

The coffee tree grows, and fruits most luxuriantly; and the tobacco plant thrives equally well. It is believed that the tea plant will yet be introduced and extensively cultivated, as it, too, thrives in that genial clime; and as for the ginger plant, and arrowroot, and pepper, &c. &c., their products are both large and of excellent quality. New Zealand flax, and many other plants of that nature, grow in wild profusion wherever introduced. Material for cordage and for paper might be produced in this new colony, had we but the labour, sufficient to supply the entire merchant service, and all the printing presses of Great Britain. The fibre of the banana plant, that grows in every garden in Queensland, is proved by recent experiments to be equal in textile value to the *musa textilus*, the plant from which the manilla hemp is manufactured. There is some difficulty in separating the fibre, but that will be overcome.

Were I to enumerate the different fruits that grow in Queensland, I should fill a very long list. The truth is, that the country, being possessed of a semi-tropical climate, is capable of growing nearly all the fruits that can be produced. I have never seen the gooseberry there, but the strawberry and the apple are introduced with moderate success. In the room of the home favourite, we have the Cape gooseberry, which is a good substitute, and is very prolific. The rosella plant yields a good preserve, much the same as red currant, with a higher flavour. The passion-fruit grows like ivy on walls and fences, and fruits most abundantly. It is of the size of a magnum bonum plum, is slightly acid, and is much relished by workmen and travellers in hot weather. It is a very common fruit, and sells for a penny or twopence per dozen. Another variety has recently been introduced, much larger, and of greater value. Apricots, peaches, and quinces grow in any quantities, but most varieties of the peach, though abundant in crop, speedily come to decay. A new variety has been introduced that suits the climate much better, and is likely to give perfect satisfaction to growers. The loquat, cumquat, guava, mulberry, mango, olive, tamarind, papaw-apple, star-apple, Bengal quince, date, date-plum, grandilla, custard-apple, rose-apple, citron, lime, lemon, alligator-pear, pomegranate, and many others, all flourish in the open air, and have the finest flavour.

But the fruits that the farmer is most likely to grow, with a view to profit, are the fig, the orange, the grape-vine, the pineapple, and the banana. The fig is a tree that soon bears, and is very prolific. At present, it is not reckoned of much value, but, I doubt not, in course of time, it will, in the dried state, become an article of export. The orange in all its varieties succeeds well, and is much prized; but, inasmuch as it grows equally well in the south, it will never become an article of commerce. Still, in such a climate, the home consumption must always be great, and instead of importing oranges, as they do now, to Queensland from Sydney, our own farmers will, ere long, grow enough to supply the demand. The climate is sufficiently warm for the grape-vine, but it grows luxuriantly, and fruits most abundantly, wherever properly cultivated. And although it cannot be considered an article of export, yet, by its plentiful production, home-made wine might be manufactured in sufficient quantities to satisfy the home demand. Some parties have commenced the manufacture of wine, and have succeeded well. It is not intoxicating, and is admirably suited to the climate. Vineyards, of considerable size, have been planted in the low country near Brisbane, and in the course of a couple of years will be in full bearing.

The fruit farmer turns his attention especially to the two fruits that remain to be noticed, the pine-apple and the banana. The pine-apple is a fruit with the appearance of which many of my readers must be acquainted; but the miserable specimens sometimes met with here give no idea whatever either of its size or flavour as produced in Queensland. The plant is most willing to grow, even though treated with neglect; and if you allow it to come within reach of soil, it rises with the vigour, and defends itself with the spirit, of a Scotch thistle. There are now many acres of pines in the different parts of the low country, and they yield a large return to the grower. The banana plant, as well as the pine-apple, is peculiar to Queensland and the northern portion of New South Wales. Neither grows to anything like perfection further south than the Richmond and Clarence; but all along the coast of Queensland they may be grown in incalculable numbers and of the finest quality. It is calculated—I have myself made the most careful calculations from data received from the grower in the midst of the banana grove—that the farmer who selects a farm of good soil, and who does fairly by his banana plants, will realize an average return of not less than £40 per acre. The expense of preparing the ground is considerable, as it should be trenched at least two feet deep before the plants are put in the soil; but such a return justifies a fair outlay, and, besides, the expense is all in preparing the ground, as the robust growth of the banana chokes the weeds that the quick soil might cause to spring up, and lessens the work of keeping the grove in order.

None but the most choice plants should be used by the farmer, and he should have them all in by the middle of June; in about 15 months thereafter he will have fruit, but the second course of fruit-bearing branches gives a much larger return. The fruiting goes on with almost no failure over a large portion of the year, and in two years and a half the grove is in full bearing. Like the pine-apple plant, the banana never fails if any portion of attention at all is given to it, and if well done by, it yields ungrudgingly such a return as can be extracted from few other agricultural products. In both cases the plant is perfectly adapted to soil and climate: this is the secret of their unfailing success.

In speaking in terms like the above of the fruits grown in Queensland, I have sometimes been met with the inquiry—" If these fruits are so productive, how is it that every farmer does not betake himself to their growth? And when their cultivation becomes general, the price must become so low as to cut off a large proportion of the high profits." My reply has uniformly been what I now put in print:—" All farmers, in selecting their farms, have not fixed on the soil that grows the banana in its perfection. All men do not cultivate the banana and other fruits with that care that secures a first-class marketable article; but principally it is to be considered that there is such a demand for pine-apples and bananas, that many years will transpire before the supply is likely to be greater than the demand. The Sydney and Melbourne markets will absorb any quantity of these fruits that the Queensland farmers can produce, though their number were augmented a hundredfold." And here, the reader will not fail to remark, lies one of the main inducements to emigrate to Queensland—its power of producing many articles in unfailing and ever-increasing demand, which no other Australian colony can produce, or produces in limited quantity and inferior quality.

Maize, or Indian corn, in all its varieties, grows luxuriantly in Queensland. The crop never fails if ordinary care is bestowed on its cultivation, although the product varies in quantity according to the seasons; and the thrifty farmer not only manages to secure some green crop between the rows in its earlier stages, but also to have two crops of corn in the 12 months. The "ninety days" variety might, indeed, give three crops in the year, if the farmer was not content with two; and the climate is so genial, and the soil so quick, that with a little planning it could be done. Maize is used chiefly for horse feed and poultry; but the finer varieties are coming into use in the shape of flour both for bread and pudding. It is very wholesome, and, though not so good as wheaten flour, is much more palatable than the Indian corn-flour which the poor Irish had doled out to them a few years ago as a substitute for the potato. Maize is grown pretty extensively, but for home consumption only; and when the farmer receives for it 4s. 6d. per bushel, he considers himself paid for the labour bestowed on its cultivation. The price is rarely below this; it generally ranges about 5s. per bushel.

A short time ago, no one would believe that wheat could be grown in this country. It seemed incredible that maize and wheat could grow within the same range of climate, and on the same soil; and yet it has been proved to be practicable beyond all dispute. The interior, however, seems to be better suited to this cereal than the coast lands. The following sentences are taken from the evidence of a gentleman belonging to the Darling Downs, given before a Committee of the House of Assembly in 1860. He states that he has grown wheat in the neighbourhood of Warwick for several years in succession, and that it might be grown on "hundreds of thousands of acres," on the banks of rivers, and over a strip of country 15 miles in breadth, extending a great many miles within the influence of the mountains:—

"Do you think wheat can be grown profitably in your neighbourhood?"

"With reference to the culture of wheat in the neighbourhood of Warwick, I am of opinion that it can be engaged in successfully. The climate is admirably adapted to the growth of this cereal, and it is altogether exempt from the diseases which are prevalent elsewhere, such as smut, blight, and rust. As far as my experience goes, I am of opinion that the growth of wheat can be profitably undertaken; for, in spite of the obstacles thrown in my way by its conveyance to Ipswich to be ground, and its re-conveyance to Warwick, I find it yields as profit—taking the average of seasons—of about 8s. per bushel when made into flour, supposing flour to be worth in Warwick £3 per bag of 200 lbs. During my experience for the last four years, the wholesale price of flour has never been under and has often exceeded that price. Maize can be, and is, grown with great success, but from the limited demand for that particular cereal this season, it is only comparatively profitable. The remarks applicable to the culture of maize apply also to barley and oats. These are usually converted into hay. There is no demand for hay in Warwick. Potatoes do remarkably well, but hitherto there has been no great demand for them at paying prices."

But even on the low country wheat grows well, and pays the farmer. Shortly before I left the colony, I saw upwards of 50 acres in one patch, growing most beautifully, on the banks of the Bremer, the principal tributary to the Brisbane, not more than 30 miles direct from the Bay; and for several years the proprietor, J. Fleming, Esq., M. L. A., states, that he has made a reasonable profit off the crop. The same gentleman, according to a colonial paper recently received, has this "year about 60 acres under wheat crop; about 30 acres are already cut and carried, and, judging from the appearance of the crop while standing, there must have been at least 40 bushels per acre on some portions of the land. The wheat is said to be of the Cape variety, but is more probably Egyptian; the head is not particularly heavy, but the straw is strong and bright. That portion of the field which, being later sown, is yet green, promises to be the heaviest crop; and if the fine weather continues, there is no doubt it will yield a fair return. A small portion, about two acres, which was sown late with white wheat, has been struck heavily by red rust, and to all appearance will be worthless. Mr. Fleming is now threshing out a portion with a very simple but efficient machine of American manufacture, worked by horse-power; with one horse he is able to thresh about 100 to 110 bushels a-day."

The successful cultivation of wheat is one of the established facts on which is based our faith in the internal and permanent prosperity of the new colony. The most sanguine of men would scarcely, indeed, calculate on wheat as an export; but is it a small matter for a colony, blessed by Providence with the power of producing many articles of export in large and growing demand in England and other countries, to be able to furnish its own flour—to provide, independent of any foreign aid, its own staff of life?

Green crops of all kinds, from the common kitchen vegetable to lucern grass for horses and cows, pay the producer remarkably well. Melons, both water and rock, of all varieties, grow with amazing quickness, and in wonderful quantities, and are used extensively by working men in lieu of water, which in this climate is not always so cool as is desirable. They make an admirable substitute, and are much more safe in hot days. An industrious man who worked for me, though he had a farm of his own, was in the habit of bringing with him a large melon, which he carefully kept from the sun, and a good slice of which, at intervals, served him instead of water. Potatoes are grown on every farm, generally in two kinds. The English potato is a very precarious crop, is much relished by the colonists, and brings high prices in such localities as Brisbane and Ipswich. Two crops are produced in the year. One in four may be good; two in four may be tolerable; one in four is a total failure. The reason of this failure is, that the root is unsuited to the climate. Still the farmers will grow it; and though they sometimes get as much as 10s., and even 14s., the hundred weight, yet it is doubtful whether the crop pays over a series of years. The sweet potato is a root differing from the English potato, and the yam of the South Seas is very nutritive, and is much more wholesome in that climate than its familiar and much-prized prototype. It takes its name from the never-failing quality of sweetness which it possesses, arising from the saccharine element that pervades it. It yields two crops also in the year; grows from vines pushed into the loosened soil, and not from roots, is very prolific when the soil is good, and is used for table, feeding horses and cows, and fattening pigs and poultry. A most valuable root is the sweet potato, although it is generally despised by new comers as pigs' meat, yet most colonists take kindly to it in a few months.

## XIX.—THREE DAYS IN THE BUSH.

Cleveland, an embryo watering-place, a few miles to the south of the point where the Brisbane falls into the Bay, is very pleasantly situated, and commands an extensive aquatic view. The magnates of Ipswich and a few of the old squatters have been bitten with a notion that the principal harbour and seaport should be there; and, some years ago, they even managed to secure a considerable sum of money with which they commenced operations. The unfinished jetty, now nearly washed away by the tide, marks the folly of the undertaking. In truth, the character of the sea-bottom is such that the revenues of the colony, for many years to come, would not suffice to make it a safe harbour for even vessels of light draught. Cleveland is some two and twenty miles from the city of Brisbane, by a road on which it would puzzle even a London Jehu to drive a four-wheeled conveyance without depositing its contents in some rut or creek. The other watering-place, called the "Brighton of Brisbane," is Sandgate, a few miles to the north of the river, also situated pleasantly, and commanding a view of the entrance to the Bay. Sandgate is some twelve or fourteen miles from the city, and the road thither is, though still in its normal condition, much better and safer than the other.

We shall return to Cleveland, whither a friend and myself set off from Brisbane on a day, above all others, unsuited for travelling in the bush. There was a succession of heavy showers, such as you rarely encounter in this country; and, though well mounted, we had some difficulty in making our way. In a few days I was to leave the colony, and the trip must either be made that day or not at all, or at least not for a long time to come. So we kept to our resolution, and braved the difficulties both of the weather and the roads. More than once we thought it a desperate undertaking, but my friend was not of the mettle to succumb.

Seven or eight miles from the city, in the midst of undulating land of a light loamy character, we drew up at the station of an old settler. It rained most heavily; we were hospitably entertained, and had a rousing fire made for our comfort. The country through which we had passed was not seen to advantage on such a day, but it seemed to grow admirable grass, and though the soil was light, much of it was capable of bearing fair crops of cotton, sugar, coffee, and fruits. The ridges were not rocky, but covered with a sharp quartzy gravel, indicative, the Victorians affirm, of the presence of gold; and the valleys between, clothed with rich grass, looked fresh and beautiful, and gave promise of a busy population ere long. We walked over the improvements on the station, which showed both enterprise and industry, and had ample evidence of the excellence of the cattle fed on these light lands. Here we met with a few families of aborigines, ensconced in huts constructed of timber and clay, the work, in great part, of the men on the station. The master informed us that he had constructed a wooden house, and told the blacks that it was for their use; but so wedded were these poor degraded creatures to their old and free habits, that they would not live in it, but preferred those miserable sties in which they were this day huddled together like so many black pigs. I have rarely found any of this race willing even to sleep in the rude wooden houses, constructed by the settlers, far less to live in them. As a rule, when they are induced to do any little bit of work on a farm, or about a house, they camp with their families some distance in the bush. At sun down they retire to their miserable twig huts, and at about eight in the morning they will make their appearance again. But it is extremely difficult to get a black fellow to work more than a few days in succession, and his daily doings are not of much value. It is hopeless to attempt to make of the black race in those parts a body of well-doing industrious men; but something might possibly be made of the children, were an effort worthy of the cause to be put forth. I have met with black children in the bush before they were contaminated by contact with the white blackguardism of the towns, who appeared in every respect as capable of being reared in the love and practice of virtuous and religious habits as any white child in the city. On the occasion of our call at this station, I had given to me the only thing in the shape of a letter or material medium of thought I have ever heard of the blacks using. The blacks, men, gins, and children are devoted to smoking, and they will do quite as much to obtain "bacco" as food. Some black wanderer near this station had been overtaken by a longing desire to obtain a bit of this wood, and he sent his request to the master in the form of a chip of ironbark, with a stick of tobacco painted on it with charcoal.

By the time we left the hospitable roof of the settler, the heavy falls of rain had swoollen the creeks, and rendered our track very heavy for the horses. Onwards, however, we pushed, and succeeded in crossing a large creek whose waters we were aware came down both suddenly and in great volume. The country was still undulating, composed chiefly of light loamy soils, and the feed was excellent. All the cattle and horses we saw appeared in good condition: in this flat country there are no sheep. As we approached the coast, the country became low, occasionally swampy near the large creeks, and was covered with most luxuriant grass. During the whole journey we had encountered nothing in the shape of timber, save the monotonous gum-tree, with a few belts of iron-bark, and box-tree on the ridges, and apple-tree and wattle on the plains. The timber, of its kind, was good, and the supply exhaustless, although much of the finest had been picked out by the wood-man. There is a great variety of timber in Queensland, much of it excellent, suited for all kinds of colonial work, and ere long it may, in some of its more valuable varieties, become an article of export. The qualities of the principal kinds have been tested by practical men, and, as placed alongside of the timber grown in the other Australian colonies and New Zealand, these stand high.

No sooner had we safely crossed the angry creek, than we began to have misgivings regarding the course we should pursue, and these were ripened into perplexity by the track which we had hitherto followed splitting into two. Each seemed equally well trodden, but they went off at right angles. To add confusion to perplexity, we were both unacquainted with this part of the bush, and the sun was near its "going down." A short consultation, and we proceeded—in the wrong direction. When we had reached the top of a low ridge, my companion reined his horse, and announced his conviction that we were on the wrong track. Drenched as we were, we dismounted, consulted a pocket-compass, and resolved to steer our way by it, through the untrodden bush, to the place of our destination. Compass in hand, we threaded our way among the great trees, and ugly limbs that lay strewed about in all directions; over ridges, across flats, through swampy places where our horses went to the girths in water, and over creeks whose depths required to be ascertained before we ventured in, we went, till at last, just as daylight was departing, we emerged on a rich, grassy, thinly-timbered plateau. In another half-hour, but not before the darkness was so dense that we could with difficulty trace the track at times, we reached the hotel at Cleveland.

In such weather no travellers are expected at bush hotels, except it be those on the main roads from the capital, inland. Very soon, however, our kind-hearted hostess (mine host had been detained in Brisbane by the weather) had a blazing fire in the parlour, and all necessary preparations were quickly made for our comfort. We must have had a wo-begone appearance. Just as we were beginning to feel the effects of the fire, and had congratulated ourselves for the twentieth time on our escape from the bush, before the dreary night had overtaken us, we were joined unceremoniously by a third party.

"Good evening, mates; this is a stormy night." We assented, as we simultaneously turned our heads towards the door.

"Not lucky to lose one's way in the bush in such a night, eh?"

"No, friend," said I.

"I've been lost all day, though, and only a few minutes ago found myself at Cassim's (the hotel keeper). Confound it, I left here this morning at eight o'clock, and here I am again."

"Where have you been? lost your way? strange your horse did not keep the track," said we.

"Confound him, when I gave him the rein, instead of taking me to the track, he turned aside to feed. I saw nothing for it, wet night though it was, but to rough it the best way I could; and as I was searching for a hollow tree where I might shelter myself from the driving rain, what should I see but a light, and making for which I was unexpectedly brought to a part of the road which I recognised, and so have found my way back to Cassim's."

We soon "knock up" acquaintance in such circumstances; it is neither the time nor the place for ceremony, and so in less than no time we became as one party. Our friend threw himself on the sofa, and left to us the monopoly of the fire. There was a good reason for this, for he, like a sensible man, had denuded himself of his wet clothes, and appeared in a snow-white suit of the landlord's; while we, like fools, retained certain portions of our dress, which we busied ourselves drying before the blazing and roaring wood fire. There was another reason that partook too much of the droll to admit of being recognised by either; and yet all parties were fully—one party perhaps painfully—aware of its existence. I have said our friend, the lost one, had put himself into a suit of pure whites belonging to the landlord. Now, it so happened that dame nature had given to our "companion in trouble" a tall athletic frame, whilst she had bestowed on mine host a very neat but rather diminutive person. How the athlete had succeeded in depositing himself in mine host's attire was to us a mystery and is so still; but the general effect was indescribably droll.

Next morning, before we were astir, our new-made friend took his departure, and we concluded that he had found his way this time as he did not return to the hotel, and no notice appeared in the Brisbane papers of a man lost in the bush. Even in moonlight it is very perplexing to travel among trees; but in a night like this nothing save the fine instinct of your horse could keep you on the track; and where that is wanting, your safest plan is to "hobble" your charger, and camp under the first hollow tree you meet with till the morning. Many a time a man bewildered will move in circles within a few miles of his destination, and, unless help comes to him, will lie down and die. You must never attempt travelling to any distance in such a wooded country as Australia without a pocket-compass, if you have not a friend to guide you; for, although you generally have the sun by day, and the southern cross by night, yet, with these helps, many an unfortunate traveller has failed to find his way, and left his bones to bleach under the hollow gum tree.

The morning was wet, and the greater part of the day was spent in looking out upon the magnificent Bay, discussing the merits of Cleveland harbour, the ministerial measures, the agricultural interest, and many odds and ends regarding snakes, and flowering plants, and lizards, and birds, and black fellows, and ants. It was not the season for mosquitoes, and somehow a colonist rarely talks about these mischievous vermin, except when they are present. Of course, we settled the question of Cleveland harbour, scrutinized with admirable discrimination all the measures before the House of Assembly, resolved that the very best thing for Queensland would be a large resident agricultural proprietary, and were very communicative on the natural history of the colony.

Snakes are very plentiful in Queensland, and the variety is great. Some of them are very beautiful, others very large, and nearly all of them seem to be all but innoxious. During my stay there, I do not remember of any fatal case, although there were many instances in which both old persons and children were bit. When a person is bit, the practice is to suck the wound immediately, and when the surgeon arrives, he generally cuts away the part wounded, and applies a cautery. The specific for snake bite is a poultice of ipecacuanha powder, wetted, and applied immediately. Nobody lives in terror of the snakes, however numerous, but every person makes it a religious duty to kill all that come across his path. In this work of reptile destruction man is greatly helped by a stupid large-headed bird, which picks up the snakes, and drops them from the tops of trees on the hard ground. They are not difficult to kill; and that work done, myriads of ants clear away the flesh in a few hours, and leave the skeleton as if it had been boiled and scraped.

The ants are an active and a scheming "people." Many times have I watched them and admired their ingenuity and incessant activity. If you wish peace, do not approach the nest of the "soldier" ant, for he is offended even with a look, and he will follow you many yards to inflict his puny spite. If you need a lesson in activity, watch the black ants as they clear away any offensive animal matter that may have been cast in the path. If you want a lesson in offensive warfare, study the tactics of the small black ant, who by his skill and tact overcomes an enemy a dozen times larger than himself. The manner is thus:—Say that a large ant has become the object of aversion to these small gentry: a dozen of them lay their heads together, and, apparently at a given signal, two fasten themselves on each leg, and in an instant the big ant, with the dozen small ones attached to his legs, is rolling in the dust.

His persecutors hold like a vice, and in vain does he attempt to rid himself of them. He rolls and tumbles about till he becomes exhausted; and as soon as his enemies dare venture to loose their hold, they do so, and, falling upon the expiring giant, cut him up into small pieces, and carry him to their nests. The white ant is an object of great aversion to some varieties of the black or common ant; and this is a fortunate circumstance, since a creature so destructive, were it not kept in check, might do immense mischief. The white ant is most destructive to the soft woods used in house building, and also to the roots of several plants. It exists in old timber, and the roots of old trees, and should it find its way into a wooden house, every particle of soft wood, such as pine, will speedily be destroyed. In a small house that belonged to me there was a wooden floor, and during four months that the house was unoccupied, these vermin did their work so thoroughly, that, when we walked across the room, our feet sank between the joists. They work in the dark and in silence; they are not half so destructive when the light shines, or when busy feet are moving about. When the white ant ascends a tree, or post, or passes from one point of attack to another, he builds a covered way in the form of a long hard tunnel which his black enemies cannot penetrate. It is when this covered way is broken by accident, or otherwise, that his enemy pounces on him and works untold havoc.

Life is wonderfully abundant in Queensland, but it is impossible for me, alike from want of preparation and want of room, to enter seriously on such an inviting subject. My remarks are casual, made almost at random, and yet they are in accordance with what I observed. Moths and beetles are very numerous, and very large and beautiful. In the season the locusts fill the forests with their sharp piercing sounds, and when rain is coming, innumerable frogs strike up a singular concert in all the hollows. Spiders spin their webs from tree to tree, and from shrub to shrub, while, high among the branches, are various birds with uncouth notes. The cockatoos and parrots of every hue and size occupy the tops of the trees. In the scrub there are many beautiful birds that are rarely seen in the bush. There are several of the pigeon species, the bower-bird, and the lyre-bird, whose plumage must be seen to be appreciated. The large birds, such as the emu, the native

K

companion, the bush turkey, the black swan, and several kinds of water-fowl, are very plentiful in some parts of the country. Many of the smaller birds that frequent the parts where the white man has raised his homestead are not destitute of musical notes, although they are not to be compared for a moment with the songsters of the English groves.

Caterpillars are very large, varied, and numerous in that colony. On one occasion, a stream of caterpillars, some of them two inches in length, passed across a portion of the Brisbane district. They were so numerous, that we could not walk along the path without crushing dozens with the foot. And, wonderful, they appeared and disappeared in the space of little more than four-and-twenty hours. There is a worm, a variety of which is found on land, and another in the brackish water, called by the colonists cobra, which plays a prominent part in the affairs of Queensland. The food and the home of the cobra, either on land or in water, is timber. It burrows in a short time into the hardest wood, and is consequently a great enemy to wooden piers and such like things. The piles that are used in such work now are all sheathed with copper to protect them from its ravages. It lives and thrives in certain kinds of trees, which it cuts through in course of time; and it so completely eats into and honeycombs the timber that falls into the creeks and impedes the navigation, that in a few months the snags form no serious obstruction to the steamer or sailing vessel. This provision for the destruction of timber falling into navigable creeks and rivers is of the highest value in a commercial point of view. While the cobra is of such service to the white man, it is of equal if not superior service to the black fellow, for it furnishes him with a much-prized food over a large portion of the year. When the worm is full grown, it is about the size of a man's finger, and is rich and nourishing; it is eaten by the blacks raw. Pray don't turn away: the black fellow eating his cobra is well matched by the white man eating his oyster.

In the afternoon the rain cleared off for an hour or two, and we set out for a place a few miles distant, where we expected to see some of the fine rich red soil that abounds in those parts, near to the coast, under cultivation. We were not disappointed, for more thriving fruit trees, and more beautifully-developed and finer-flavoured fruit, I certainly never met with in Queensland. The land had been all trenched two feet deep, and according to appearances, and the account of the manager, the proprietor would be repaid in a very short time. The view from this part commanded a large sweep of the Bay, with Moreton and Stratbrook islands in the distance, and St. Helena about ten miles off. We were informed that the proprietor was about to build a mansion here; and certainly he could scarcely find a site more desirable, in many respects, on all the Bay.

Next day we set out for Brisbane, but such a quantity of rain had fallen, and the creeks were so flooded, that we found travelling rather a difficult task. In many parts of our track the water was knee deep; some parts it reached our saddle-flaps, and at one place we were compelled to wait four hours before it was safe to venture our horses in the boiling and tumbling stream. At last we ventured, and with difficulty reached the opposite bank. While waiting for the falling of the waters, a black fellow came up, and entered at once into conversation. We wished him to swim our horses and ourselves across, and offered him some money. He looked askance at the money, but fixed his black eye on a carriage rug thrown over my shoulders, and said, "Me do it for that fellow blanket," pointing to the rug. "Bale," said I, "that fellow blanket goes with me to white fellows' country." "Ah!" said our black friend. We coaxed him, and urged him, and gave him silver, which he took, and said, if "white fellow come to another fellow ford," he would take us over. We went, and we returned again, but in vain did we urge him to take the water. By and bye he left us to our meditations, and then we saw that in the transaction we, the "white fellows," were "gammoned" by the cunning black.

## XX.—POPULATION, COMMERCE, REVENUE, AND BANKING.

It was in December, 1859, that Queensland commenced its separate existence. The district of Moreton Bay, the name by which it was known when a portion of New South Wales, as alleged by the residents there, was subject to much neglect for many years by the central Government at Sydney, and therefore the start was not made in the most favourable circumstances; and yet at its commencement, Queensland took, in a financial point of view, a high place in the scale of British colonies. The population was limited for such a territory, being, as near as could be ascertained at the date of separation, 30,000 inhabitants to a country at least nine times the area of England and Wales. It was the custom at that time for those who were opposed to separation to assert that the population was much lower; but the returns which have reached this country prove that the northern men were nearer the mark in their numbers than their opponents; and they prove also that the population of the new colony is rapidly increasing. The census returns of 1861, give the population as upwards of 31,000; and now (1862), it must have reached 37,000.

The following table will show the progress of the population. The entire population in the Moreton Bay district, now Queensland, in

| | |
|---|---|
| 1846 was | 2,257 |
| 1851 ,, | 10,000 |
| 1856 ,, | 17,082 |
| 1861 ,, | 31,000 |
| Now (1862) the numbers may be | 37,000 |

In 1856, the town population amounted to 8,500, as near as could be, the half of the whole; the remaining half were distributed over the country. About 4,400 were resident in Brisbane, 2,500 in Ipswich, and the remainder in Drayton, Warwick, Dalby, Gayndah, Gladstone, and Marybourgh. The proportion between town and country will, in the present census, in all probability, be found to be about the same when the returns are completed. It is believed that since 1856 the population of the capital has nearly doubled. Great, however, as has been the increase in the past years, it is not the standard by which to judge the probable increase in the future. We may reasonably anticipate a large flow of the most suitable kind of emigrants from the mother country to Queensland, as soon as the capabilities and attractions of the colony are known; and even now the colonial papers show that every week brings to Brisbane from the other Australian colonies no less than 100 men, four-fifths of whom have come to try their fortune in the new colony. These men are generally the very best immigrants, for they have already learned colonial experience in the other colonies, and most of them bring some capital. I have already mentioned this fact as one of the most conclusive arguments in favour of Queensland as a field for British labour.

Brisbane is the capital and the principal seaport. Ipswich is the largest inland town, and is situated about 25 miles from Brisbane, on the road to the Darling Downs. Warwick is a town on the Condamine, in the southern division of the Downs, and near to the boundary of New South Wales. Here the telegraphic wire from Sydney joins the wire from Brisbane by Ipswich. The distance from the capital is about 100 miles. Drayton and Toowoomba, two inland towns, within three miles of each other, are situated in the eastern portion of the Downs, near to the Main Range, and comprise about 2,000 inhabitants. Toowoomba is the more recent and the more thriving of the two, and occupies a commanding position. It is about 85 miles from Brisbane. Dalby is a small town in the Northern Darling Downs, and is distant from the capital about 140 miles. Gayndah lies much further north, at the head of the Burnett district, and is about 220 miles distant from the capital. From the thriving town of Marybourgh, 150 miles to the north of Brisbane, and the seaport for the Burnett, Gayndah is only 85 miles. Marybourgh is situated about 60 miles from the mouth of the Mary, which falls into Wide Bay. This is an important town, and between it and Brisbane there is regular communication by steamer. The population may be at present about 1,000; but inasmuch as it is the very heart of the cotton-growing country, it will, doubtless, rise rapidly in public favour. On the east coast there are two more towns, and a third will speedily rise in the new district of Kennedy, on the Burdekin. The two yet to be named are Gladstone, in the Port Curtis district, 260 miles north from Brisbane; and Rockhampton, 45 miles from the mouth of the Fitzroy, and about 350 miles from the capital. Canoona gold diggings are about 40 miles above Rockhampton.

Between Brisbane and Marybourgh, Port Curtis, and Rockhampton, steamers run regularly once a fortnight; between Brisbane and Sydney, Melbourne, and Newcastle, once a week; and between the capital and Ipswich, two or three steamers ply daily. There is besides a good road between the two chief towns, on which the royal mail coach runs twice a-day. The bush roads are generally mere tracks, but in the neighbourhood of towns the process of road-making is progressing with kindred things. Tramways, constructed of the hard wood of the colony, are about to be tried between the capital and the Downs, and great expectations are raised in connexion with this mode of transit. The telegraph will, in a month or two, connect the chief towns in the south of Queensland, and these with Sydney, Melbourne, and Adelaide. There is also a telegraphic wire between Brisbane and the pilots' station on the Bay. These modes of transit and communication, in operation and in progress, in a colony so recently raised to its political independence, speak strongly for the practical wisdom of the legislature, and the sound-headedness and enterprise of the people.

The following extract is taken from a pamphlet published in Brisbane, in January last, by the editor of the *Moreton Bay Courier*:—

"The trade of Queensland is at present confined to the neighbouring colonies and the mother-country, but it must be remembered that we are only just 'commencing business on our own account,' and we must, therefore, be content gradually to enlarge the sphere of our operations. The imports into the port of Brisbane alone, in the 12 months ending 30th September, 1860, amounted to £561,496; but the total value of the whole imports into the colony during that period is estimated at £650,000. This sum was principally expended in bread stuffs and other articles of consumption, including spirituous and fermented liquors, and in drapery, hardware, furniture, imported stock, &c. &c., as the subjoined recapitulation of imports into Brisbane will show:—

| | | | |
|---|---:|---:|---:|
| Fermented and spirituous liquors.. | £36,944 | 4 | 0 |
| Agricultural produce .............. | 68,799 | 12 | 6 |
| Live stock........................ | 7,460 | 0 | 0 |
| Assorted merchandize ............. | 448,293 | 0 | 0 |
| Total................... | £561,496 | 16 | 6 |

"It is within the range of probability, however, that the second item will be considerably reduced, ere long, by the local production of many of the articles we are now compelled to send money out of the country for; and it is in this, as well as in other particulars, that we expect benefit to accrue from the proclamation and settlement of the agricultural reserves referred to in the last chapter.

"The great bulk of our exports consists of articles connected with pastoral pursuits, and this will continue to be the case until cotton or some other valuable staple is counted among the number. The total value of the whole exports from the colony of Queensland, during the 12 months ending September 30th, 1860, was £573,372 3s. 6d., and in this amount wool—the principal product—figures to the extent of £415,397 11s. 9d. —the value of 13,564 bales; while hides, tallow, sheep-skins, and live stock, make up a further sum of £124,238 16s. The aggregate amounts of both imports and exports show a balance in favour of the former of upwards of £120,000, and some might be led to suppose that we are in a crippled condition because the 'balance of trade' is against us; but we have a multitude of examples in our favour in this respect. Such circumstances are only incidental to the infancy of a state; and no harm can accrue if our exports be found to be steadily increasing. That such is the case, we can show by quoting the value of the exports from Brisbane alone during the four years ending with 1860, thus—

| | | | |
|---|---|---|---|
| 1857 | £355,237 | 14 | 0 |
| 1858 | 363,513 | 17 | 0 |
| 1859 | 429,984 | 3 | 0 |
| 1860 | 435,744 | 1 | 9 |

"As long as this steady progress is observable, an occasional deficit need excite no cause of apprehension; for, as the exports of a country increase in value, so must there be a corresponding increase of material and national wealth."

In recent papers received from the colony, we find the revenue summarised by the editor of the *Queensland Guardian*, on the occasion of the Colonial Treasurer's Financial Statement to the Assembly, and we shall transcribe a portion of the article. The budget seems to have been most satisfactory, and received with general approbation. The writer goes back to the commencement of our colonial existence, as the reader will perceive, and thus gives a fuller view of the subject:—

"The colony of Queensland, having commenced her career in the close of the year 1859, began at that time to receive into her own treasury the ordinary proceeds of taxation and other revenue, and these, for the short portion of the year which then remained, amounted to £6,475 17s. 8d. The expenditure for the same period involved the payment of several liabilities which had been incurred before separation, and which were, therefore, due from the New South Wales Government. Our outlay, thus swelled, amounted to £8,689 10s. 7d.—exceeding our income by £2,213 12s. 11d. This deficit, however, does not exceed the sum paid by us for New South Wales; so that if that colony had liquidated the claim, as she was bound to do, we should have had no deficit at all. As it is, she has merely given us a promise to pay when the inter-colonial account is squared up, and we are, therefore, compelled to deal with the item, in the meanwhile, as a bad debt. (There is a further sum of over £18,000 received by New South Wales, which ought to have been paid into our treasury. In this amount New South Wales also acknowledges herself indebted to us. Thus, had matters proceeded in regular order, we should have had a considerable balance in our favour at the end of 1859.)

"The amount for 1860 then opens with an entry on the wrong side of £2,213 12s. 11d. The estimated receipts for that year were £160,000, and the expenditure £149,319. Instead, however, of £160,000, the sum of £178,589 8s. 5d. was that actually received; while the expenditure was swelled by supplementary estimates to £161,000, which, with the previous year's deficit, amounted to £163,213 12s. 11d. This left a balance of £15,375 15s. 6d. on the right side of the account, with which to commence 1861.

"For this year the estimated revenue is £182,200; and the expenditure, as originally provided by the Government, £197,663, to which, however, have been added supplementary estimates to the amount of £24,370 1s. 8d., making in all £222,033 1s. 8d., or £39,833 1s. 8d. more than the estimated receipts. It will thus be seen that our revenue will have to exceed the estimate by more than 20 per cent., in order to meet the requirements of the present year; and when we remember that the estimate for this year is only £3,000 or £4,000 over the amount received last year, whereas our receipts for the past single month of April have exceeded the whole receipts during the first three months of 1860—we may, without being very sanguine, conclude that such will be the case.

"For next year the ordinary revenue is estimated at £225,700, and the expenditure £210,545. In addition to this, it is proposed to borrow the sum of £115,300 (for the construction of permanent works), to be provided for by a sinking fund, and paid off in 12 years. It is a bold, and will be thought by many a foolish thing to say, that it would afford us no surprise to learn from the treasurer's statement two years hence that the ordinary revenue for 1862 had proved more than sufficient to meet this demand without touching the loan."

From this necessarily brief statement regarding the revenue of Queensland, it will be observed that trade is gradually expanding; that the funds are very sensibly growing; that the Government is liberal in the expenditure of money on permanent works for the general good; that there is no great disposition on the part of any to borrow; and that all parties are inspired with hope for the future. Nor can it be said by any person who has read this little work thus far, that that hope is ill founded.

I shall add a little tabular matter, regarding the banking interest in Queensland, which business-men will love to ponder, but which the general reader may skip, if he likes.

*General Abstract of the Average Assets and Liabilities and of the Capital and Profits of the under-mentioned Banks of the Colony of Queensland, for the Quarter ending 31st March, 1861.*

No. 1.—LIABILITIES.

| Banks. | Notes in Circulation. | Bills in Circulation. | Balance due to other Banks and to Branches. | Deposits. | Total Liabilities. |
|---|---|---|---|---|---|
| | £ s. d. | £ s. d. | £ s. d. | £ s. d. | £ s. d. |
| Australasia | 12,157 8 4 | 1,604 5 2 | ...... | 84,744 17 0 | 98,506 10 6 |
| Union of Australia | 8,558 16 8 | 1,060 19 0 | ...... | 97,852 19 0 | 107,472 11 8 |
| Australian Joint Stk | 12,505 16 8 | 224 1 0 | ...... | 65,749 10 11 | 78,479 8 7 |
| New South Wales | 13,753 10 0 | ...... | 52 18 1 | 62,494 19 4 | 76,301 7 5 |
| Totals | 46,975 11 8 | 2,889 5 2 | 52 18 1 | 310,842 6 3 | 360,760 1 2 |

QUEENSLAND;

No. 2.—ASSETS.

| BANKS. | Coin. | Landed Property. | Notes and Bills of other Banks. | Balance due from other Banks, and from Branches. | Notes and Bills discounted, and all other debts due to Banks. | Total Assets. |
|---|---|---|---|---|---|---|
| | £ s. d. | £ s. d. | £ s. d. | £ s. d. | £ s. d. | £ s. d. |
| A. ...... | 20,088 7 11 | 4,650 0 0 | 265 18 4 | ...... | 236,786 0 4 | 261,841 15 1 |
| U.A. ... | 11,525 17 6 | 1,980 0 0 | 151 18 4 | 5,374 10 8 | 131,004 18 4 | 150,037 4 10 |
| A.J.S... | 14,946 7 11 | 6,082 9 3 | 143 2 6 | ...... | 70,302 6 2 | 91,474 5 10 |
| N.S.W. | 19,664 10 0 | 1,523 8 4 | 729 16 8 | ...... | 70,802 0 7 | 92,719 15 7 |
| Totals.. | 66,225 3 4 | 14,235 17 7 | 1,290 15 10 | 5,374 10 8 | 508,895 5 5 | 596,073 1 4 |

The Bullion in the Bank of Australasia is £51 8s. 6d.

No. 3.—CAPITAL AND PROFITS.

| BANKS. | Capital Paid up. | Rate per annum of last Dividend. | Amount of Dividend. | Amount of Reserved Profits at time of declaring Dividend. |
|---|---|---|---|---|
| | £ | | £ s. d. | £ s. d. |
| Australasia .................. | 900,000 | 12½ per cent. | 56,250 0 0 | 315,043 3 3 |
| Union of Australia ......... | 1,000,000 | 12 ,, | 60,000 0 0 | 213,847 5 0 |
| Australian Joint Stock ... | 375,000 | 10 ,, | 18,730 0 0 | 29,114 13 3 |
| New South Wales ......... | 750,000 | 15 ,, | 55,954 15 0 | 207,934 7 10 |
| Totals.................. | 3,025,000 | | 190,934 15 0 | 765,939 9 4 |

The above tables are extracted from the *Queensland Guardian*, and the editor of the paper affixes the following note:—

"A comparison of this return, with that published in our Summary of February, gives satisfactory evidence of our monetary stability. It will be seen that the deposits have been augmented by the sum of £22,925, and the advances made by the banks by £41,823. As almost the whole of the latter increase is furnished by the English banks, while the additional deposits may fairly be ascribed to new arrivals in the colony, it is manifest that the confident reliance placed by ourselves in the resources of Queensland is now being shared by the foreign capitalist."

## XXI.—THE DUGONG FISH—THE MEDICINAL QUALITIES OF ITS OIL.

In an early chapter of this work, I mentioned the dugong fish, and promised to give the reader some account of its nature and habits. The dugong has been long known to the blacks in the north as a fish whose flesh was good for food, and whose fat was possessed of extraordinary healing powers. They were in the habit of spearing the creature in the shallow water of the bays along the coast of Queensland, roasting the body in a hole made in the sand, and, in devouring the delicious flesh, they took care to rub their persons with the grease. A few years ago Dr. Hobbs, health officer at Brisbane, was led to try the effects of the dugong fat, or oil, in cases where cod-liver oil was generally administered by the faculty, and to his surprise and delight, found that it did not simply possess qualities equal to those of the cod-liver oil, but added several of its own, and these of the highest importance to the invalid. The nature of the creature, the remedial qualities of the oil, and the class of patients to which it may be given or applied, I shall allow the discoverer to describe in his own language. I shall only add that I have seen and examined the creature, and that most of the cases mentioned by Dr. Hobbs in his published lecture on the subject, and several not mentioned there, were parties whom I personally know in the colony.

Quoting from "Knight's Animated Nature," Dr. Hobbs states, that—

"The dugong (halicore dugong, Cuvier) is a native of the Indian seas, being common among the islands of the Indian Archipelago, and visiting also the coasts of New Holland. Its favourite haunts are the mouths of rivers and straits between proximate islands, where the depth of water is but trifling (three or four fathoms), and where, at the bottom, grows a luxuriant pasturage of submarine algæ and fuci. Here, in calm weather, may small troops be seen feeding below the surface, and every now and then rising to take breath. The position of the mouth, the muscular powers, and mobility of the lips, garnished with wiry bristles, and the short incisor tusks of the upper jaw, enable these animals to seize and drag up the long fronds of subaquatic vegetables which constitute their nourishment. The dugong is in high esteem as an article of food, its flesh being tender and not unlike beef; hence it is assiduously hunted by the Malays, who attack the animal with harpoons, in the management of which they are very dexterous. The mutual affection of the male and female is very great, and the latter is devoted to her offspring. If a dugong be killed, the survivor of the pair, careless of danger, follows after the boat carrying the body, impelled by an overmastering passion, and thus often shares the fate of its partner; indeed, if one be taken, the other is an easy prize. The dugong attains to the length of seven or eight feet. In Moreton Bay they are frequently met with nearly twice that length. So sweet and palatable is the oil procured from the dugong, that in its *pure state it may be taken* without disagreeing with the most sensitive stomach, and also used in a variety of ways in the process of cooking; so that this potent restorative remedy may be taken as food, and many ounces consumed almost imperceptibly every day, and thus furnish the system with the requisite amount of carbon for its daily oxidation.

"The beneficial effect of dugong oil in chronic disorders in general may be attributed to its nourishing properties, the blood being supplied through the chyle with absolutely necessary ingredients, without that stimulation of the system which almost every article of diet will, more or less, produce. But in chronic disorders of the digestive organs, in the treatment of which it is peculiarly valuable, I am inclined to the opinion that, in addition to its emollient action upon the digestive mucous membrane, the unusually large proportion of glycerine this oil contains, exerts its peculiar solvent powers upon the crudities and inspissated bile locked up in the alimentary canal, which by their presence keep this highly sensitive membrane in a perpetual state of irritation. This irritation, if not relieved, soon becomes reflected in some of the numerous organs connected with it by nervous communication; thus, the windpipe, the lungs, the heart, the liver, and the kidneys become at first only sympathetically affected, and, if overlooked, ultimately the seats of fatal organic disease.

"I was first led to the use of this oil by having under my care a young man who had suffered from an obstinate obstruction in the bowels, terminating in acute inflammation, for which he had been bled five times, and otherwise extremely reduced, leaving him in an exceedingly debilitated condition. His illness extended over a period of eight months, and the debility attending the stage of convalescence was very protracted, notwithstanding the administration of all the usual remedies prescribed in such cases, together with every necessary comfort. Feeling assured that, owing to the irritability of the stomach of my patient, cod-liver oil could not be retained if administered, I resolved upon trying the dugong oil as a substitute, telling him not to expect any great improvement until he had taken it for a month. At this time he was so weak he could not walk from his chair to the verandah of his house, a distance of a few yards only, without experiencing the distressing feeling of exhaustion. In a fortnight, under its use, he could take short walks; and in a month could leave his house for several hours, walking a considerable distance without feeling much fatigue. He then went to the bay, and amused himself in fishing and procuring this oil, which he used freely, not only in its pure state, but also frying his fish and flour-cakes and other articles of food in it. He returned to see me in perfect health, and quite fat. It was not the mere recovery of this patient that so much surprised me, but the *rapidity of the change* from complete prostration to perfect health and vigour."

The importance of this remedial agent justifies me in devoting a little space to these extracts; for, suppose this oil to possess all the qualities attributed to it by Dr. Hobbs, who has used it in an extensive practice for several years with marvellous success, then it must be an incalculable good to bring it under the notice of invalids, and those of the medical profession who may chance to read these pages. The following facetious description of the creature and its habits, the means by which it is taken, and the manner of preparing the oil, is furnished by Dr. Hobbs. It is extracted from an article entitled "Submarine Squatting in the new Colony of Queensland:"—

"Upon the island of St. Helena, in Moreton Bay, the first submarine run has been formed, and is now in the second season of its operations, under the superintendence of an experienced person formerly engaged in the seal trade in Newfoundland. Around this lovely island, for miles in every direction, are extensive sub-marine pastures of great luxuriance, affording a never-failing supply of long grass, and upon which the herds of dugong feed and fatten like oxen on the plains; yet unlike them in requiring no stockman to tail them, no stockyard to confine them, and no driving to the abattoirs.

"The habits and physical conformation of this curious marine animal, corresponding in so many particulars with the description of Behemoth by the patriarch (Job. xl., 15), have led some to the belief that the two are identical. Such belief, however, is not without some show of reason. The Egyptian word from which the name is derived (Be-he-mo-ut), signifying *water-ox*, strongly supports such an idea, and this is coupled with the facts that the digestive apparatus of the dugong is precisely alike in every particular to that of the ox, and the bones so heavy, that, from their great weight and density, when struck together they give out a metallic sound, thus closely agreeing with the scripture description before referred to, 'He eateth grass *as an ox*,' 'his bones are like bars of iron.' Whether this supposition be right or wrong, the dugong has as good a claim to the honourable mention of the patriarch, as the hippopotamus (sea-horse), which animal has generally been considered the behemoth.

"For seven months in the year at least, from September to March, these animals are taken almost daily, by means of long nets set across the channels leading to and from their feeding grounds. The nets used are of considerable length and depth, and of large mesh, such as were formerly used by deer stealers in days gone by, and such as were probably used, if there be any truth in the legendary story, by Henry VIII. in securing the portly old friars of Waltham Abbey on their midnight travel to Cheshunt nunnery, and who, when captured, were complimented by the royal polygamist as being the fattest *bucks* he had ever taken.

"The boiling down operations are continued without any interruption during this period. A large boiler, capable of holding one of those monsters, is continually steaming away, and the oil flows away from a tap in the upper part of the boiler in a clear limpid stream, of the colour of pale sherry wine. Upon cooling, the oleine and stearine separate, the latter being retained in the flannel bags through which it is filtered, and is sold to the soap-makers for about £40 per ton; while the former is used for medicinal purposes, and is consequently of great value, being used by Dr. Hobbs and other medical men as a substitute for cod-liver oil, and has been found as serviceable in every malady attended with debility as that popular remedy. The steady and continuous demand for this oil, both from England and the neighbouring colonies, is sufficient proof of its utility, and of the position it is likely to assume in the catalogue of our colonial exports.

"The flesh of the dugong is considered by those who have tasted it a great luxury. From the same animal can be procured flesh resembling beef, veal, and pork. It appears to be a highly nutritive kind of food, for not only do the natives, but the white people also, who engage in the pursuit of capturing them, and consume it in the absence of beef and mutton, become remarkably fat. Upon a submarine station there need be little expenditure for beef and mutton. The submarine squatter who can dine off a veal cutlet fried in oil every day, cannot complain much of his cuisine, for even Soyer, with the most perfect gastronomic arrangements, would fail in supplying a more dainty dish, concerning which an American writer has said, 'It was a dish of which Apicius might have been proud, and which the discriminating palate of Heliogabulus would have thought entitled to the most distinguished reward!'

"There is no part of this animal which does not possess a commercial value. The bones, particularly the ribs, 18 in number on each side, when carefully boiled and freed from the oil they contain, cannot fail to be of considerable value from their great weight, density, and resemblance to ivory, being free for the most part of cancellated structure."

In appearance, the dugong is a creature between the seal and the whale, with a head resembling that of a fat calf. The one I saw dissected on St. Helena was about nine feet long, and of great girth over the shoulder. It carried a large quantity of flesh. The white men engaged in the fishing are quite as fond of the flesh as are the blacks; and even our party had dugong steaks to breakfast. What between the dugong, the various kinds of fish, the oyster, and the turtle, that abound in all the bays that indent the coast, Queensland waters are likely to be as productive of wealth as Queensland soil.

## XXII.—QUEENSLAND POLITICAL AND SOCIAL.

There are no great political parties in colonies such as those that divide public men at home, simply because there is the absence of great questions on which the colonial mind is divided. There is, indeed, diversity of opinion, plenty of it; but this does not arise so much from opposite views on a given subject, as from the views of the different parties being more or less advanced. Thus politicians of all shades call themselves liberal, although the more advanced may sometimes twit the more cautious with conservatism. When one arrives in the Australian colonies, he fancies the most conservative organs of opinion far advanced in radicalism, and for a time he marvels on what grounds there can be any "opposition party" either in the Legislative Chambers or in the public press. By and bye, he finds that there is; and he discovers also that the grounds of opposition are sometimes of a very trivial nature, and apparently the opposition waxes the more loud and stormy in proportion to the narrow space that separates the two. The political manifestations of the older Australian colonies within the last few years have not favourably impressed the home mind; but, perhaps, these are not so much the indications of chronic disease as incidental irritations and distempers which time and experience will purge from the body politic.

Queensland politics have hitherto been peaceful, and the "coach" has neither been upset nor much jostled. The vehicle is of a good make, with nearly all the improvements in political coach-building; but the steady progress it has made is mainly owing to the driver and the guard. The speech of His Excellency the Governor, at the opening of the first Legislative Assembly, was more than an average specimen of such productions, and the ministerial programme was cautiously drawn up. To an on-looker, the first responsible Ministry in Queensland seemed less inclined to realize their own ideas, than they were anxious to ascertain the real import of public opinion, and to embody it in law. Hence, on several occasions, when important measures were criticised and discussed by the "opposition" in the House, or by the public press, they were not deaf to remonstrance, nor backward to introduce amendments. Some men may call this weakness, pusillanimity, and so forth;

we believe that this reasonable spirit of accommodation and compromise was the thing that chiefly contributed to the unwonted success of the session. There was no ministerial crisis; several important measures were discussed without reserve, without the indulgence of party feelings, and passed into law; and when the session came to a close, men were surprised at the amount of real work accomplished.

In the first session certain modifications of the laws under which Queensland came into political existence were effected, to suit the new circumstances. It might be expected that all parties would unite to accomplish such an object; but it showed not a little courage and confidence in the purity of their motives, and a refreshing determination to do their duty, when the representatives of the people, led on by the Ministry, undertook the settlement of such questions as these:—The Land Laws, as they bore on Agriculture and on the great Pastoral Interest; Education, both in regard to primary schools for the benefit of all classes, and higher schools for the benefit of those whose parents might desire for their children a higher education than could be derived from the former; and the vexed question of State Aid to the Church. It may be supposed that on such subjects a diversity of opinion would prevail in the Assembly; and, as the *Times* said at the reception of this news in England, "it was something for the first assembly of a new colony even to entertain such questions." But not only were they entertained, they were fully discussed, and Acts passed in the case of each, more liberal and more just than those in existence on the same subjects in the older colonies, by such decided majorities as shall deter any man or Ministry endowed with common sense from intermeddling, unless it be to make the measures still more perfect.

The measure on Education embodies the national idea, and the object is to have all the children educated, so far as that can be done, without being exposed to the curse of sectarianism. Denominational schools, by coming under certain conditions, receive certain pecuniary advantages; but the public feeling is undoubtedly in favour of one great national system, free from the denominational element as far as that can be effected. The system is in the hands of a Board fairly representing the different religious parties, and it is worked by an efficient inspector.

It has made a good start, although the heads of the English and Romish Churches are understood to be opposed to it. In colonies, Bishops have not so much power as they have at home, and therefore we may hope to see the great problem of teaching the people on a system quite unsectarian soon solved in Queensland. The measure regarding the Church is simply of this nature—that no grants of money or of land shall henceforth be made to any section of the Christian church, but that all sections shall be left to carry on their own efforts by means of the contributions of the people. The claims of those parties, however, who had shared in the money grants given by the Government of New South Wales previous to separation, were respected; and, consequently, each clergyman retains the same till his death or removal from the colony. The sum paid annually is £750. The Governor, in his address at the close of the first session, congratulated the members of both Houses on the settlement of this vexed question.

The admirable character of the land laws must have often appeared to the reader as he perused these pages. I need say nothing more of the new squatting laws than what has been said under the head, "How to secure a 'Run.'" And the laws that apply to lands previously under lease are equally reasonable. The Act for the "Alienation of Crown Lands" is the one with which most of my readers may have to do, for it is in accordance with it that sales of the public lands are regulated. "Under this law the public lands are divided into three classes—town, surburban, and country lots; the former comprising all land within the actual boundaries of towns; the second, all land within two miles from the nearest boundary of any town (the Governor, with the advice of the Executive council, having a discretionary right to narrow this limit in certain cases); and the third class, all other lands whatsoever." The price of land sold under this Act is in no case less than £1 an acre, and the lots must be properly surveyed and delineated in the public maps before the alienation from the Crown can be completed. The auction system is resorted to in all cases, except as regards the agricultural reserves, in respect to which the right of free selection at the upset price is permitted; the terms of purchase at the sale being—10 per cent. deposit, and the remainder within one month afterwards.

"The Act prescribes that, within a period of six months after its passing, reserves to the extent of at least 100,000 acres shall be proclaimed for agricultural purposes 'on the shores or navigable waters of Moreton Bay, Wide Bay, Port Curtis, and Keppel Bay;' and, further, that, within five miles of all towns whose inhabitants number more than 500, reserves of 10,000 acres shall be set apart with a like object. The same clause also authorizes the reservation of land in other localities, but the power thus given to the Government is purely discretionary. Farms upon these reserves are not to be less than 40 acres, or more than 320, and persons desirous of procuring them must apply at the office of the Land Agent (who is generally the Clerk of the Petty Sessions in the district) nearest to the reserve, and there point out on the map the lot or lots they may wish to select; the amount of the purchase-money, at 20s. per acre, must then be paid down—either in current money, or in the 'land orders' they may have received from the Government on their arrival in the colony. The settler must go to work upon his farm, and commence to improve and cultivate it, for, if this condition be not fulfilled within six months after the purchase, then the money is to be returned, less 10 per cent., and the farm reverts to the Government.

"The occupant of a farm may lease lands contiguous thereto on such reserve to the extent of three times the quantity owned by him—providing that the whole does not exceed 320 acres—at an annual rent of 6d. per acre. The lease may extend to a term of five years, but the lessee has the power during the time of purchasing any part, or the whole, of the land so held by him, notwithstanding the application of other intending buyers, he having a pre-emptive right to the same. The land so held, however, must be fenced in within eighteen months from the commencement of the lease, under penalty of forfeiture; and it is also forfeit if the rent be allowed to run more than 30 days in arrear. No sub-letting is permitted, nor is it competent for any person to borrow money on the security of such lease."

The summary just given we have extracted from the pamphlet before quoted. But, in addition, there is the important clause in this Bill that authorizes the grants of land to emigrants. According to this clause, any person from England, or any European country, paying his or her passage out (men under 40, and women under 35), is entitled, on landing, to a "land order," worth £18, for which you can take up, on any of the agricultural reserves you like, 18 acres of as good land as you can choose, and, at the end of two years, the same party is entitled to an additional land order for £12. Each adult is entitled to land orders, value in all £30, and the passage-money, as advertised, is £18. Every two children in a family, under 14 and above four years of age, are entitled to the same amount of land, on the condition of paying the passage-money. There is no restriction as to age when the parents are accompanied by not less than five children. Thus, the head of a family, consisting of father, mother, and six children, between the ages mentioned, will have, on landing at Brisbane, or any other port in Queensland, placed in his hands five land orders, each worth £18, and for which he may select 90 acres of the finest land in the colony; at the end of two years, he has placed in his hand other five land orders, value £12 each, with which he may purchase 60 acres more. Thus, one family of the size mentioned will, at the end of their second year in the colony, be in possession of 150 acres of good agricultural land—a perfect fortune to a working-man's family. Mark this, too: the emigrant to Queensland *selects* his own land; is not compelled, as in New Zealand, to take what falls to his lot, whether it be good or bad. The power to select is an immense boon; for, in that case, you can have your land anywhere, and either town, suburban, or country land, as you choose, according to the value of the "orders."

The emigrant to Queensland has, therefore, a liberal grant of land, on terms that enable him to make the most of it; he has the prospect of a thorough education for his children; and he is neither dunned for taxes, nor exposed to have his "goods seized and sold for conscience sake." Grants of money for religious purposes, which occasion so much discord and bitterness in the other colonies, do not exist there; and, consequently, while he has plenty of this world's goods to enjoy, he "sits under his own vine and fig-tree," in perfect peace, and worships the God of his fathers without distraction.

The form of Government is the same as that which obtains

in the other colonies. The Governor is appointed by the Crown, and is its representative in the colony. There are two Legislative Houses, the Assembly and the Council. The former consists of 26 members, and is elected by the people; the latter consists of 14, and is at present nominated by the Crown, that is, by the Governor, as the representative and embodiment of royalty in the country. But the representatives of the people, with the consent of the Council, have the power to make the Council elective. The Executive consists of three members, Colonial Secretary (Premier), Treasurer, and Attorney-General, appointed by the Governor, with seats in the Assembly, and responsible to the people's house. The only qualification for membership is, that one's name should be on some electoral list. Thus, the highest offices in the colony are open to all able and meritorious men. No man in holy orders is eligible. The elective franchise is virtually manhood suffrage, as the conditions are within the reach of all industrious men. A man, to exercise the franchise, must be 21; he must possess a freehold worth £100; or, rent a house or farm at not less than £10; or, hold a pastoral licence from the Crown; or, be in receipt of £100 salary per annum; or, pay £40 a-year for board; or, £10 per annum for lodging. In a colony like Queensland, every industrious man may exercise the franchise under one or other of these qualifications, and few, indeed, are excluded, save criminals, and those who have fallen into arrears of rent or municipal rates.

Brisbane, Ipswich, and several other towns have sought incorporation, and have consequently been proclaimed municipalities, having a mayor or chairman, and a body of aldermen or councillors as in English boroughs. The qualifications that entitle a man to vote for a member of the Assembly entitle him to vote for the list of councillors. The powers entrusted to the municipalities are large, and are intended to operate in behalf of the community. To carry out their plans, they may rate all lands, houses, &c., within the municipal bounds, as well as borrow money; and during the first five years of their corporate existence, Government grants an equal sum to that raised from the rates. In succeeding years, the proportion of the Government grant graduates down to nothing. In this, as in all new countries, the municipal authorities have plenty of work to do, and they have been quite late enough in commencing. In towns where the population increases rapidly, such as Brisbane, it is all that they can do to keep pace with the general progress.

The aspect of colonial towns, especially when in their earlier stages, is very different from what we see at home. Melbourne and Sydney have, indeed, quite an English appearance; but such towns as Ipswich and Brisbane, being principally composed of wooden houses, look new and strange to an Englishman. In Brisbane, however, many of the old strange-looking houses are now giving place to buildings of brick and stone, of a very substantial character, and more approved architecture. Most of the banks occupy spacious buildings, and several of the merchants and shopkeepers are not behind them. And there are some very excellent private residences rising in various directions; but the greatest architectural effort that has been put forth is the new jail, that cost upwards of £22,000, and the finest building is Government House, which is now in progress, and will cost somewhere about £15,000. There are several neat buildings belonging to the various sections of the Church. The Roman Catholic, the Episcopal, the Presbyterian, and the Baptist churches are of stone; the Wesleyan and Independent are of brick. The latter is stuccoed and washed a light stone colour, and, from its fine proportions and commanding position, is one of the chief ornaments of the city. The design is by the Colonial Architect, a gentleman whose fine taste is becoming conspicuous in the rising city. There are besides the buildings connected with the National School, the School of Art, several hotels, &c. &c.

In Queensland there are seven newspapers, all professing liberal principles, and all of them conducted with a tolerable amount of ability. The defects and faults incident to a new society are conspicuous in some of these journals, but these are being rectified by the good sense and manly bearing of the people. The postal arrangements are liberal in Queensland. Letters delivered in any town where posted, are 1d.; letters sent to any part of the colony, are 2d.; letters sent to any of the other colonies, or England, are 6d., all pre-paid. Newspapers go free, except those to England, which are charged one penny.

Society is just forming in this new colony, and for a time it must, of necessity, assume a crude and unsettled character; but there is in Brisbane, and in all the towns, a large amount of the proper elements of which society is chiefly composed—honourable, intelligent, and virtuous families. The Brisbanites are well-to-do in the world, are a very hospitable people, and are conspicuous for their benevolent efforts and Christian liberality. Nowhere, so far as my knowledge extends, do people contribute more largely and more freely to the support of religious worship, and to the temporal support of those who may, by accident or death, be deprived of their means of living, than they do in Brisbane. Many of the people are fond of reading, and there is a tolerable supply of books, but whether the reading there has just got into the channels, through which the greatest amount of good is derived, is a question which I shall not presume to decide. The people generally are busy all the day, and when night comes, are scarcely fitted for much close mental exercise, and hence reading naturally verges towards the light and easy. There is there, as in most places, where people do congregate, a desire for pleasant entertainment, such as concerts and lectures; but there is not a marked tendency towards the frivolous. There will be found there, of course, as well as in other towns, some who love the light and frivolous; but these are well kept in check by the moral influence of the body of the people. The working classes are in a most favourable position, and have every chance of rising in the social scale. Many of them are becoming wealthy in their land, and cows, and horses; and some, as might be expected, miss the opportunity, grow indolent, regardless of self-respect, sink into loose habits, and disappear, or turn up after a time as a moral nuisance. There are many who rise—there are some who sink; and if, on the one hand, the rise be rapid, so is the sinking process. Some men cannot stand prosperity, although they have for years braved most manfully the severe storms of adversity; and when they frequent the bar of a public house, or tipple in their own houses, the descending process is surprisingly rapid, and the end is certain ruin. An unprejudiced person would, however, give a favourable report of colonial society, especially in towns where the numerous humanising and softening influences are allowed to operate. In the bush there are many privations; men are removed from many moral and spiritual restraints; and who can wonder if their morals should be lax, and their behaviour rude? But yet in the bush I have met with as much hospitality and honest manly feeling as one can meet with anywhere.

## XXIII.—THE CHURCH, IN TOWN AND IN BUSH.

There are no time-honoured institutions in the Australian colonies. There is nothing connected with the aborigines to revere. There are no old and touching associations, no grey ruins to remind us of any primitive faith, however erroneous, or primitive worship, however rude. All things are new; the mind feels free from all ecclesiastical traditions, and attaches small importance to ecclesiastical forms. But in colonies generally, whilst "traditions" and "forms" have small influence, there is no lack of deference for, and homage to, practical religion. The reality is highly prized by many; but, of course, there are many others, who, like Jeshurun of old, "wax fat and kick." God blesses them with prosperity, and they cease to acknowledge their dependence on Him, vainly imagining that their own arm had brought them what they have. But those in whose heart the truth and love of God dwell, stand out a noble contrast to the others, and by their active and useful lives prove to all "whose they are and whom they serve." The line of demarcation between professors of religion and non-professors may be more distinctly drawn than in home society; but the genuine element is not less rare, nor is it less potent and practical, than in England. We draw this conclusion from various facts. The Sabbath day is as well kept in the towns in Queensland as it is in the mother country, and a great deal better than in many parts; the attendants upon the services of the Church are very liberal in their support of public worship; the benevolence of the people is really great and much to be commended. Now, after all, the religion that is worth the name, the religion that we most desire in Queensland, is that which manifests its presence, not by controversy, but by love and charity; not so much by a sharply defined creed as by a holy life; not so much by metaphysics as by goodness.

No man can estimate the importance of the religious element

when pure and vital, when a living power, and not a dead letter, to a country at the commencement of its career. It is one of the elements that should enter into, nay, that should permeate, the foundations of a nation. What would England be without her religion? without its vital power, permeating all society, where would be her strength? without its fruits in the lives of men, where would be the moral beauty that she presents to the world? England's true greatness rests on her religion; remove the one, and the other will decline and disappear. No people will ever be truly great if they are not religious. The country that lacks the pure and loving religion of Jesus Christ is destitute of the main element of permanent success. This element must influence and mould the character of the people. It must not be handled by the civil power; it must live and work in the hearts of the people. That is its field; there it will gain its trophies; and thus shall men do all work, political, mercantile, social, in the spirit of that holy religion. A nation may support churches by votes of money, and you may have a gorgeous ecclesiasticism covering the land; but there may be no life in it, or the life may be a source of strife and bitterness. Let the men of whom the nation is composed fear God and honour His laws, and you have in that nation a fountain of honour and goodness, whence issue constantly the streams of noble principle and loving action. God Himself hath said, "Them that honour me I will honour;" and God is not honoured by a haughty formalism, paid and pampered by the State, but by the unfeigned homage of a People's heart, and the peaceful loving actions of a People's life. The religion that is received and supported thus; that moves to kind and charitable actions; that breathes the spirit of brotherly love; that does to all men as it would wish all men to do to it; *that* is the religion that "exalteth a nation," and *that* is the religion which finds its home, not in State-created systems, but in the humble hearts of believing men.

I speak now against no Church; my part is to speak the feeling of the body of the people of Queensland regarding the religion which they desire and which they are prepared to support ungrudgingly, under whatever Church polity it may appear. What they want is a principle that will lead them to God in His own loving way through Jesus Christ; a principle that will elevate their minds and purify their hearts; a principle that will cheer and comfort them in the land of their adoption; a principle that will bind them closer and closer in happy brotherhood; a principle with which they may regulate their life, and, when God pleases to call them away, on which they may rest comfortably in death. And whatever Church presents this principle, it will be received without much ado regarding the polity by which that Church may be regulated. The truth is, they would have the reality, and care less than people at home generally do for the form in which it is embodied.

The kind of clergymen best fitted for colonial work, therefore, are men who, though they must needs profess some special ecclesiastical connexion, yet reckon it their main object to teach and enforce the great principles of our holy religion, rather than to dwell on church formulas, or stir the waters of ecclesiastical strife. The man who does not pique himself on his Church connexion, who does not fall back on tradition or human authority, who does not seek "honour" as a clergyman, who does not endeavour to rise at the expense of his brother, but who goes like a man and a brother among the people, takes a respectful interest in their affairs, sympathizes with them in their sorrows, rejoices with them in their joys, tells them in an honest manner the truth of his mission, and, in firm but kindly language, points out their faults—*this* man shall be respected, and obeyed, and supported. The people generally are honest and straightforward, however much they may sometimes err; and if they are met in the same spirit by a clergyman, they appreciate these qualities, and honour the man who possesses them. But your whining, sentimental, demure novice of a clergyman, they will certainly treat as this miserable caricature of the man and the minister deserves. It has been the custom among more sections of the Church than one to send men whose hopes of success at home had all but expired to the colonies, thinking perhaps that anything was good enough for them; but never was there a greater mistake, never a more serious blunder committed. The men who emigrate in our day are among the most intelligent and enterprising of their respective classes; these men in many instances constitute a congregation in a colonial town, not surpassed for the power of appreciating a good sermon by any congregation in any of the towns at home. It is, therefore, a grand mistake to send such men, the refuse of your home clergy, to minister to them in spiritual things. Why, the best men that enter the home ministry might well feel honoured to be called to God's spiritual work among the population of which the colonial communities are composed; and as to the work itself, what can be more important than laying the foundation on which the spiritual superstructure of a great nation is to be reared?

It seems to me that into all Churches that wish to prosper in Queensland the lay element should be introduced, and allowed free exercise within defined limits. The spirit and temper, and I might say the intelligence, of the people are such, that it might be done without any anxiety. Besides, when the Church has no connexion with the State, and receives no money grants therefrom, but is dependent on the free-will offerings of the people, there are many reasons why the laity should take their share in the business affairs of the Churches. Possibly some readers of this little work may demur to such suggestions as these. I have no controversy with you, my friends; all I attempt is to tell you candidly what is the state of feeling generally in that colony in regard to matters ecclesiastical, and to counsel you as to the course most likely to be successful. I am sure of this—the clergymen who have the least priestly spirit about them, and the Churches which allow the free exercise of the lay element, are the clergymen (other things being equal) who shall have greatest influence for good—are the Churches that shall take the deepest hold on society. Give the people the Christian liberty which is their inheritance; trust them in all matters ecclesiastical, as you do in all matters political; let them have the man of their choice; and it matters not to which section of the Church he may belong, I tell you the people there will hold him in due respect, and they will cheerfully contribute to his support. My own experience is, that a more liberal, honourable, and considerate people could not be easily found in either hemisphere.

All the sections of the Church nearly are represented in Queensland. The most numerous section is the Church of England; the next is the Roman Catholic; and the four sections, Presbyterians, Independents, Wesleyans, and Baptists, may be said practically to be about equal. Of the Episcopal

Church there are one bishop and ten clergymen; of the Roman Catholic Church there are one bishop and about six clergymen; there are five Presbyterian congregations with ministers; four Independent; four Wesleyan; three Baptists; one Lutheran; and one Primitive Methodist. At the time we write there are at least 36 clergymen engaged in ministerial work in Queensland, in a population consisting of 37,000 souls. The entire system of public worship is conducted on the Voluntary Principle, with the exception of six ministers who held office before separation, and who had distributed among them annually £750 of Government money. In no part of the colonial world with which we are acquainted is there better provision for the spiritual wants of the people—one clergyman to every thousand of the population. This is not amiss for the voluntary principle. It is indeed a grand experiment; and we trust that the people of Queensland will stimulate each other to love and good works, and prove to the world that the free-will offerings of the worshippers constitute an ample revenue for the Church's wants.

The opponents of the voluntary principle argued in the late discussion, that whilst it might possibly provide the means of religious instruction for the towns, it could do nothing for the bush. The opposite was proved at the time; and it would not be out of place to state a few things here on this question— the Church in the Bush.

First, the statistics of the various colonies showed that what money was granted by Government to the support of religious worship was nearly all expended on the populous districts; a very small proportion indeed in connexion with any Church participating in the grant was expended on the bush. Secondly, in the colonies generally, and in Queensland especially, nearly all that had been done to carry religion to the thinly populated parts of the country was the work of the voluntary principle, and generally the agents were connected with and supported by the Churches who receive no aid from the Government. Thirdly, squatters, and other gentlemen connected with the bush, have shown a willing and liberal disposition to contribute their money to provide for the religious wants of the people far removed from towns. The only thing that was not forthcoming was the suitable men for the work, and these no

Government can supply. Fourthly, the system that is required for the bush is one of itineracy, the agents of which should be men of robust health, fair education, liberal and tolerant in their religious views, and of a manly spirit. Two or three sections of the Church might contribute to the support of such a system; or each Church might do its own endeavour in that way. Already we observe the Bishop of the English Church is instituting some such agency as this; and for some years the Presbyterians, the Independents, and the Wesleyans, have been practically engaged in the work. The complaint has never been lack of money, but want of the properly qualified men.

The religious condition of Queensland will stand a fair comparison with that of any colony receiving money and land grants in aid of public worship; and, what is more, in some respects it will not suffer by a comparison with many parts of our own highly-favoured England. I am aware that sentiments directly opposed to these have been expressed on the platform, and issued through the press, by parties high in office, and that the English public has been extensively appealed to in behalf of the spiritual destitution of the Queenslanders. I was in the colony when this scene was being acted in England, and I can tell you that the reports of the speeches that reached us there filled the people with surprise and indignation. Queensland needs men of the character and type above described; and if England will supply the agents, I am bold to say the men and women in Queensland will supply the money.

## XXIV.—EDUCATION.

I shall not insult the understanding of my readers by telling them that the education of a people is one of the weightiest questions that can engage the attention of the moralist and the statesman. In an old country like England, it is involved in numerous and all but insurmountable difficulties. There are so many interests to be respected, so much diversity of opinion to be met, so many prejudices to be mollified, that men are deemed more courageous than wise who talk of the establishment of a system catholic in its spirit and national in its operation. Hitherto, our greatest statesmen and our wisest moralists have failed. It is a vexed question, and whether it will ever find a solution in England is more than the most sagacious will affirm.

In the older Australian colonies, rival systems, as in England, have unfortunately been introduced, and both are supported on a liberal scale by the respective Governments. Scattered over the colonies there are a few schools in a prosperous condition, that are conducted by competent persons at their own risk, which receive no aid from Government; but, generally speaking, the schools are either ranged under the term "denominational" or "national." The former is thoroughly sectarian, and ostensibly used for sectarian purposes; the latter is catholic, and has to battle against many powerful prejudices. How the two antagonistic systems work, and what are their respective results, in the older colonies, it is no part of my duty to describe; and it is enough for my present purpose to state, that, from the experience of the older colonies in the matter of education, the Queensland Government and Legislature were led to decide, after due deliberation, that the system best suited to the infancy of the new colony was the one most catholic in its spirit, and universal in its application. The terms "national" and "denominational" were both discarded, and two Acts were passed establishing a General System of Education, including both Primary and Grammar Schools, on the basis of the National System, and admitting of pecuniary help to existing denominational schools on certain conditions. The intention of the House, and perhaps of the Ministry, was to establish and support a purely national system, into which the existing denominational schools might be gradually, and by a friendly process, absorbed. But whether this most desirable object shall be gained is rendered extremely doubtful, by the strong denominational likings of the Bishop of the English Episcopal Church. Every friend of peace—every man who desires to see the rising race and future generations in that promising colony trained in the principles of mutual forbearance and brotherly love—must wish success to the system of general education now established in Queensland.

During the first session, the Parliament voted the sum of £10,000 for the purposes of education, £7,000 for primary schools, and £3,000 for the grammar schools' foundation. This may appear a very small sum for such a purpose, but it should be considered that the population of the colony did not at the time much exceed 30,000 souls.

The Act to provide for primary schools, which is the one of greatest importance in the present state of the colony, is, as we have said, based on the national system, and the object is to furnish a good education to all the children throughout the colony as far as these can be reached. The system is managed by, and all the property connected with it is vested in, a Board, consisting of six persons, including the chairman, who must be a Minister of the Crown, representative of the Government in either House. The appointment of the Board lies with the Executive. The powers of the Board are great, but subject to control. It makes rules and bye-laws for the working of the system; but the Act fixes that those shall be in accordance with the spirit of the "National System of Education," and they must have the approval of the Governor, and be laid before the House of Assembly. Schools, whether denominational or private, may have pecuniary aid, provided they submit to the supervision and inspection of the Board, and in all things conform to the authorized rules and regulations; but no money is granted for the purpose of building, unless the fee-simple of the property is vested in the Board. Should the inspector not be satisfied that the assisted school is conducted in accordance with the regulations of the Board, on representation made to the proper quarter, the aid is withdrawn. The books in use at present are those used in the National Schools in New South Wales. These include the volumes on the Old and New Testament; but dogmatic or doctrinal religion is imparted by the clergyman to whom the children belong ecclesiastically, or by any person authorized by the parents in his place, at certain fixed hours, according to the convenience of the parties. The Government profess to provide the best education procurable, and they have given every facility for the religious instruction of the children by those whose duty it is to impart it. In any district where there are 30 children not attending any school, the parents of those children may combine and ask the establishment of a school in connexion with the Board. The conditions of success are these—that they subscribe one-third of the actual cost of the buildings, the Government give the other two-thirds, and that they appoint from their number a local Board to manage the school when in operation. The local Board may recommend a teacher but the appointment is in the hands of the General Board. The salaries of teachers are regulated by the work to be done, and afford a fair remuneration. The system has made a good start, and already in all the chief centres of population schools are established. All depends on the working of the scheme, and if we may judge from the composition of the Board, we may believe that the party in power as well as His Excellency the Governor are most desirous that it may be worked well and efficiently. Parents emigrating to Queensland may therefore feel assured that all that the Government can do to provide a good education for their children is being done; and we have no doubt, from what we have seen of the Queensland system in its commencement, that if not intermeddled with by the "heads of denominations," it will work admirably, and confer an inestimable boon on the industrious community; and should the Governor, the Executive, and the Board stand firm to the grand principle to which they are pledged, the hearty sympathy and support of the people will more than counteract the persistent opposition of a dozen bishops.

Here and elsewhere in this work I have been led to speak freely of the efforts of certain parties in the colony, who, from mistaken views, I doubt not, have used their influence, and we believe are still using it, to subvert or nullify some of the most enlightened and most statesman-like measures of the Colonial Parliament. The reader will observe that not a word has escaped my pen condemnatory of the men or the offices they fill; but I hold that those, whatever be their office, and whatever be their motives, who seek to evade the conditions and nullify the spirit of such vastly-important measures as those that the Legislature of Queensland has passed on the church question and education, are guilty of acts that merit the severest reprobation; and should the guilty one, as in this instance, fill the sacred office, I know of no code of morality that would justify me, a man pledged to speak the truth and deal fairly by every man, in allowing the sacredness of the office to change the character of the act. Let bishops, judges, and all men observe the Golden Rule, and respect the laws under which they live, and none will be more forward than ourselves to give "honour to whom honour is due."

## XXV.—EMIGRATION, EMIGRANTS, WAGES, HINTS, PRINCIPLES.

Those who have read the preceding sections of this work will, I dare say, feel with me that little more requires to be said on emigration. That it has been good for many families that they were led to emigrate; that many more would really benefit themselves much were they at the present time to cross the seas; that of all the excellent colonies connected with the British Crown, Queensland is the most excellent and the most attractive to the industrious working man and the small capitalist; that now, when emigration to America is all but stopped, and our cotton supply from the States disturbed and uncertain, every legitimate effort should be made to direct the flow of British emigration to England's own Cotton Field:—all this will be granted by every candid mind. It would benefit all parties were the tide which is now rising to set in with a vigorous and steady flow towards Queensland; and if what I have stated regarding that new country be true, which it *is*, it matters little to which of the Australian colonies men may be induced to go: if they have a ten pound note left in their pocket when they land at Melbourne or Sydney, the chances are that they will find their way to Brisbane.

Will you take advice from one who has nothing in the world to gain or to lose by your going to one colony rather than to another, but who would wish you to go to the healthiest and the most productive? If you resolve to emigrate, unless you have friends in the other colonies who are willing and able to give you a start, take ship direct to Queensland. In this way your expenses in going out are reduced by £8 or £10 each adult, and you secure the very liberal grants of land which the Queensland Government give to every adult, and every child above four years of age. The general character of the country; the nature of its soils, and its climate; its unequalled resources; the ways in which you may be employed; the probabilities and the conditions of success, have been faithfully, though imperfectly, placed before you. I have also shown you that the laws of the colony are liberal and wise; that religion and education are well provided for, the one by the people, and the other by the Government; and that the body of the colonists are industrious, prosperous, and happy. It lies with you to decide.

There is a steady demand for labour of most kinds. In the interior, the demand exceeds the supply. Shepherds, ploughmen, masons, carpenters, wheelwrights, blacksmiths, are always needed; and for many others, such as saddlers, shoemakers, tailors, painters, quarrymen, plasterers, labourers, printers, bricklayers, tinsmiths, upholsterers, grooms, &c., &c., there is a fair demand. There is no class of emigrants more required and more certain of immediate employment at high wages than female domestic servants of *good character*. There is in Queensland, as in all the other colonies, a sufficient supply of clerks and shopmen; and there is no opening whatever for educated men of no trade or profession without capital. Clerks and shopmen who are prepared to put their hands to any work that may turn up, will succeed; but your man of education, incapable of doing any manual labour, and possessed of no income, is the most helpless and hopeless of all colonists. I have sometimes heard people say of such cases, "Such and such a one should go to Australia; he will surely find something to do; there must always be plenty to do in a new country." This is true as regards the industrious, well-principled workingman of any trade, who is both able and willing to put his hand to any kind of work; but it is *not* true as it regards a well-educated, penniless, handless, and, therefore, in a colonial sense, *useless* man.

### *Current Wages in Brisbane.*

Stonemasons 11s. to 12s. per day.
Bricklayers, 11s. to 12s.
Carpenters and Joiners, 8s. to 12s.
Plasterers, 11s. to 12s.
Painters, 8s. to 10s.
Blacksmiths, 10s. to 14s.
Masons' & Bricklayers' Labourers, 6s. to 8s.

Quarrymen, per day of 10 hours, 8s. to 9s.
Labourers, 6s. to 9s.
Tinsmiths, £2 to £2 15s. per week.
Upholsterers, per day, 9s.
Female Cooks, £26 to £36 a year.
Tailors (piece-work).
Saddlers, 8s. to 10s. per day.

Milliners, £40 to £80 per annum.
Dressmakers, £30 to £60.
Needlewomen, £30 to £40.
Shoemakers, a-week, £2 to £3.
Coopers, per day, 15s.
Printers (Compositors), 1s. 3d. per 1,000.
Printers (Pressmen), per day, 10s. to 12s.

Shepherds, a-year, with rations, £40 to £60.
Grooms, ditto, ditto, £35 to £60.
Farm servants, do., do., £35 to £40.
Married couples, with services of wife, double rations, £52 to £85.
Servant maids, a-year, with board and lodging, £18 to £25.
Bullock drivers, ditto, £35 to £45.

The following paragraph is extracted from a document issued under the authority of the Colonial Government:—

"Persons with the bare means of existence at home, but who can manage to pay their own passage out, will find themselves in the possession of a farm immediately on their arrival in this colony, and may enter forthwith upon the cultivation of the soil with the fairest prospects of success. Others who may not be possessed of any capital, on their arrival in the colony may be certain of immediate employment at good wages, with board and lodging, and the amount they can save out of their earnings in two years will be quite sufficient to enable them to enter upon their own land, to the whole amount of which they will then be entitled in the proportion of £30 worth for each adult, and half that amount for children between the ages of four and fourteen years, if they have paid their own passage out; or to £12 worth for each adult, and half the amount to children, if they have been conveyed to the colony free of expense to themselves."

Since my return I have frequently been questioned on certain points:—First, as to the supply of water. Queensland is very well watered, as the reader must have observed; and with ordinary care, every squatter and farmer may have a sufficient supply of fresh water all the year round. In this respect it contrasts favourably with the colonies to the south. There are not many running springs, and few wells as yet have been sunk, but what between the fresh-water creeks and holes, and the tanks that are now being made in connexion with every respectable house and farm, there is no lack of this important element. It is rendered pure, if need be, by passing it through a filter, and it is kept cool by shading it from the sun. Considerable anxiety has sometimes been manifested regarding the floods that occasionally visit some districts. On this point there need be no anxiety, for in Queensland they have never done much damage. Some have also got the notion that the rainy season in Queensland is unfavourable for the picking of the cotton. This, too, is a mistake, as in the southern portion of the colony, at least, there is no decided rainy season, the rain being distributed over a larger portion of the year than in the other colonies. For the same reason, Queensland is not visited, except at long intervals, with anything in the shape of droughts. In a general sense, the colony of Queensland is well watered. There is a greater number of rivers there, navigable for many miles, than will be found in any other Australian colony.

Secondly, as to the feeling of the blacks. Over Queensland there may be distributed, in tribes, between 20,000 and 30,000 natives of the soil. In some districts they are troublesome, but, generally speaking, they are inoffensive. I have never known the blacks to be the aggressors; but, when injured by the whites, their revenge may slumber, and it may not fall on the head of the guilty, but it will come, and sometimes with terrible consequences. My belief is founded on the experience of many as well as my own, that, if you act in a humane and judicious manner towards the poor degraded blacks, both your person and your property will be safe. It is sad to think that these poor creatures are melting away before the march of the white men, notwithstanding all that may be done by individuals and by Government to contribute towards their comfort. Every effort to civilize and christianize them has failed; and even the attempts that have been made to teach and train the young have invariably come to naught. Whether this may have been owing to the incorrigible roving disposition that pervades all the tribes, or to the hurtful influence of that portion of the white population with which they mainly come in contact, or whether it may be owing to both these causes combined, I shall not attempt to determine. But the fact is as I have put it. The blacks need not be a bugbear to any intending emigrant, and as for the other difficulties that may rise in his path, they are nothing in comparison with the advantages that are his for the taking.

Thirdly, as to the best timber for use. The emigrant who resolves to settle on the land will have much to do with timber, and it is a matter of some practical importance to him to know which of the timbers may best suit his purpose. Timber is required for house-building. The posts on which the framework rests should be of bloodwood, and generally all the timber that goes into or comes in contact with the soil; in the absence of which, iron-bark, or the hardest kind of gum-tree, may be used. Two objects will be gained by this arrangement—the foundation of the house will stand longer, and it will be impervious to the white ant. The walls of the house should be constructed of broad slabs split from the iron bark-tree, and placed in strong grooves, either upright or on their sides, according to the taste of the builder. The rafters may be of any saplings that grow conveniently; the covering may be sheets of bark of the stringy-bark tree, or shingles made of the iron-bark tree. The bark when well cut and neatly placed, forms a perfectly impervious roof, but the best covering is the shingle roof. The bark is taken from the tree standing, and as much may be gathered in a day or two as will serve the purpose. The blacks may sometimes be got to gather the bark for a couple of shillings. The doors and windows should be made of pine, a timber plentiful and easily worked, but not so durable as the home or Baltic pines. A handy man may construct both doors and windows. Glass is cheap. The house should have a wooden floor, but it should be of some of the hard woods, as the pine falls a speedy prey to the white ants, if any nests of that feeble but destructive creature be within reach. The chinks in the wooden walls serve as ventilators during two-thirds of the year, and should the inmates experience the least inconvenience, a lining of calico will prove an infallible remedy. I have more than once been asked—But what is a family to do after reaching their freehold farm before the house is erected? For eight or nine months in the year the climate is so fine, that a family will suffer no injury were they for a few nights to spread their couch on a bed of reeds or grass, sheltered on the side the wind might come from, and over head by a blanket. Timber is also required for fencing. Fencing should commence with clearing; and it may be that the timber you require to cut down in order to bring the ground under cultivation may supply you with the stuff for fencing. In the south of Queensland, that is, the country near Brisbane, there are three kinds of timber good for fencing. There are others besides, but it is enough for all practical purposes to refer to these. The posts, which are morticed when green, should be of bloodwood if possible; but if that timber is scarce, iron-bark may be used. Always use iron-bark for rails when it can be had, and in its absence either bloodwood or spotted gum. Both posts and rails are made of split wood, and are heavy. The former are let into the ground about 18 inches, and firmly rammed. The fence generally consists of three rails, which are let into the posts. The expense of erecting such a fence, which will last for 20 years, is from 5s. 6d. to 7s. per rod. But small proprietors do their own fencing at intervals, as they do their own clearing.

Fourthly, as to the leasing of land, and the condition on which land in the agricultural reserves is sold. The condition of sale is that the land purchased at £1 per acre shall be taken possession of and improvements commenced within six months. This is to prevent the land-jobber from buying up the good lands. The farmer may have on lease, at the rent of 6d. per acre per annum, land contiguous to his farm, not exceeding 320 acres; and he is entitled during his lease to purchase any part or the whole, if the same shall have been fenced. Should the rent not be paid regularly, or the land not be fenced within eighteen months after the lease is taken, the lease becomes void.

Much depends on the principles and disposition of the emigrant. A discontented, grumbling, envious man is not likely to find himself very comfortable even in Queensland; and the man of lax or doubtful principle, though he possibly may grow rich, is not likely to rise to positions of honour and influence. In colonies, as well as in the old country, all men trust the person of unquestioned honour and unsullied morals. A man is removed from many wholesome restraints in a colony that operate most beneficially on him at home; therefore all who emigrate should keep alive within them every virtuous feeling and principle, and, wherever situated, should attach themselves to some Christian church. Allow me, therefore, to say, ere we part, that the man who carries with him to Queensland and retains the unimpeachable honour, the open manliness, the robust morality, the unostentatious generosity, and the liberal vital Christianity, which characterise the best of Englishmen, is the man whose presence is specially needed there, and who shall, in a very short time indeed, become a power in the infant community.

# APPENDIX.

## I.—CONDITIONAL GRANTS OF LAND FOR COTTON CULTIVATION.

Colonial Secretary's Office,
Brisbane, July , 1861.

His Excellency the Governor, with the advice of the Executive Council, and in accordance with Resolutions of the Legislature, is pleased to declare that the following Regulations for the granting of suitable portions of land to persons or companies undertaking the cultivation of cotton, shall have the force of law from and after the 1st day of August, 1861.

By His Excellency's command,

Robert G. W. Herbert.

### Regulations.

1. The land to be held by any one person or company under these Regulations must be comprised within one block of not less than 320 nor more than 1,280 acres.

2. The situation and general boundaries of the land applied for must in the first instance be notified to the Surveyor-General; and the Government reserve the power of refusing to grant such land, as for public reasons it may be deemed unadvisable to alienate in the manner herein provided.

3. On the approval of an application, the applicant must deposit in the Treasury, in Brisbane, the amount of 2s. for every acre applied for, and on such amount being duly deposited, an authority to occupy the land will be issued, subject to the conditions hereinafter mentioned.

4. Should the land not already have been surveyed for sale, the application will only be approved of conditionally until the

survey has been duly completed in accordance with the rules of the Survey Department, and by a surveyor to be approved by the Surveyor-General, and such survey shall be at the sole cost of the party applying.

5. If, within two years from the date of the authority to occupy, the occupant shall produce to the Commissioner of Crown Lands for the district, or such other officer as the Governor may appoint, satisfactory evidence that at least one-tenth part of the land has been planted with cotton, and that a sum in the proportion of at least £5,000 to 640 acres has been *bonâ fide* expended in clearing, fencing, cultivation, or improvements connected with the production of cotton on the land, the deposit of 2s. per acre will be returned, and a deed of grant in fee issued to the occupant.

6. But if, at the expiration of two years from the date of the authority to occupy, the occupant fail to produce satisfactory evidence of said expenditure and cultivation, the amount of deposit will be forfeited, and the land, together with all improvements thereon, revert to the Government; provided that in the event of the sum expended and the land under cotton crop being not less than one-half the amount required by the aforesaid Regulations, the occupant may defeat the forfeiture of the land by paying the amount of £1 for every acre not duly covered by such expenditure as aforesaid, but the deposit of 2s. per acre will be absolutely forfeited.

7. No Land Orders will be issued as a bonus for the production of cotton on land held in occupancy under these Regulations, until the conditions entitling the occupant to a deed of grant have been fully complied with.

8. No applications to occupy under these Regulations will be received after the 1st day of August, 1863, unless by special notice in the *Government Gazette*, extending the period for the receipt of such applications.

## II.—NEW IMMIGRATION REGULATIONS.

The following are the new Immigration Regulations as adopted by the Legislative Assembly of Queensland:—

1. That the "Remittance System" of Immigration, as in force in Queensland until the commencement of the present year, be resumed, and that the payments to be made thereunder be as follows:—For each immigrant between 1 and 12 years of age, £2; between 12 and 60, £4.

2. That persons desirous of engaging servants or labourers under the "Guarantee System," specified in clause 9 of the existing Regulations, be permitted to pay a portion, not being less than £6, of the passage money of such immigrants upon their arrival, and the remainder during the first year after such arrival; in the event of the balance not being paid, the original payment, together with the land order, to be forfeited.

3. That land orders be divided into two classes, those delivered to persons sending for labour or for their friends or relatives to be at once transferable; and those delivered to immigrants or persons paying the passage of immigrants under clause 7 to be transferable after six months, and not earlier, unless specially sanctioned by the Immigration Board.

4. That all transfers of land orders be dated and signed by the party transferring them in the presence of, and attested by, a Justice of the Peace of the Colony.

5. That upon application from the Board of Education, the Government provide intermediate or cabin passages for certificated schoolmasters or mistresses of a superior class.

## OUTFITS AND VOYAGE NECESSARIES.

The Emigrant should exercise both care and caution in selecting all that he requires on the voyage and on his first entrance upon colonial life. There are those who, in their several branches of business, devote much attention to these matters. Messrs. Monnery & Co., the eminent Outfitters, supply Clothing and all Cabin Necessaries; and we cannot but direct attention to the comfortable, light, ventilating Hats, specially made for warm climates, by Messrs. Ellwood & Co., who have obtained a Prize Medal at the Exhibition. Messrs. Tupper & Co. supply Iron Houses, Sheds, Roofs, &c., carefully packed for shipment; and Messrs. Wilson & Co. supply Cotton Machinery, for which they have also obtained a Prize Medal. The Advertisements of these Firms will be found at the commencement of the Work.

THE END.